The Official YALSA
Awards Guidebook

Young Adult Library
Services Association
a division of the
American Library Association

THE OFFICIAL

YALSA
Awards
Guidebook

compiled and edited by

Tina Frolund

for the
Young Adult Library Services Association

u Ottawa

Neal-Schuman Publishers, Inc.
New York   London

Published by Neal-Schuman Publishers, Inc.
100 William St., Suite 2004
New York, NY 10038

Printed and bound in the United States of America.

The paper used in this publication meets the minimum requirements of American National Standard for Information Sciences-Permanence of Paper for Printed Library Materials, ANSI Z39.48-1992.

Library of Congress Cataloging-in-Publication Data

The official YALSA awards guidebook / compiled and edited by Tina Frolund for the Young Adult Library Services Association.
     p. cm.
  Includes bibliographical references and indexes.
  ISBN 978-1-55570-629-6 (alk. paper)
  1. Young adult literature—Awards—United States. 2. Young adult literature—Bibliography. 3. Teenagers—Books and reading—United States. 4. Young adults' libraries—Book lists. I. Frolund, Tina. II. Young Adult Library Services Association.
Z1037.A2O38 2008
011.62'507973—dc22

2008017584

Contents

Foreword

In 1999 I was working for the Kansas City (MO) Public Library. I had been a professional librarian for just over three years at the time. That year the library's young adult specialist was a member of YALSA's (Young Adult Library Services Association) Best Books for Young Adults (BBYA) committee and was moderating several teen input sessions focused on BBYA nominations. It was at one of these sessions that I first heard teenagers' comments about Walter Dean Myer's *Monster* (HarperCollins, 1999). I had read the book but had not yet talked about it with any teenagers until that session. Early in the discussion it became very clear how deeply affected many of the teens had been by the book. I can still clearly recall the comments of one 14-year-old young man. When given the opportunity to share his thoughts, he did not jump out of his seat with excitement. He did not wave his hand in the air wildly to grab anyone's attention. He said, simply, "I read this, the whole thing. I really did. I stayed up all night to finish it. It was really good." He didn't say anything more. Several teenagers nodded their heads in agreement and understanding. His brief comments had captured exactly how they all felt.

Months later in January 2000 *Monster* was named YALSA's first Michael L. Printz Award winner. It has received much well-deserved critical acclaim over the years, has been the subject of many teen literature discussions, and, along with the 2000 Printz Honor books *Skellig* by David Almond (Delacorte Press), *Speak* by Laurie Halse Anderson (Farrar Straus Giroux), and *Hard Love* by Ellen Wittlinger (Simon & Schuster Books for Young Readers), helped to set the highest standards for YALSA's Printz Award in defining "literary excellence." But it is the straightforward, poignant comments delivered by that 14-year-old young man those many years ago that have always remained with me. His words remind me that YALSA's award books connect with teenagers in a unique and enduring way. These are complex and groundbreaking titles that are read by teenagers not once but again and again, providing something new each time. These are the books that cause young adults to offer that strongest of teen endorsements, "I read this, the whole thing. It was really good."

It is no easy task for the librarians serving on the various award selection committees to find these books, those titles that fulfill their committee charges and also connect with teenagers. YALSA award selection committees consist of a wide variety of members representing many different communities. Some are from multibranch public library systems serving cities and large metropolitan areas. Others are from school libraries serving students in small, rural communities. Award committee members read hundreds of books and spend hours discussing titles. In order to complete their task these diverse members must come to a consensus about what book or handful of books best fits the criteria for their specific award.

Serving on one of YALSA's prestigious awards committees is a great privilege and a tremendous responsibility. The hard work of these committees and their members matters greatly. People from around the country and the world—librarians, teens, teachers, reporters, and many others—wait with great anticipation for YALSA's annual January announcement of the award-winning titles. Minutes after the announcements the impact of YALSA's work is clear. Booksellers and libraries see a quick reaction from the world with sales of award winners increasing almost immediately and library reserve lists for these titles growing lengthy overnight.

The excitement of the annual announcement, however, should not overshadow the insight that the history of YALSA's awards can provide about the growth and expansion of teen literature. For example, the winners of YALSA's longest-standing award, the Margaret A. Edwards Award (established in 1988), cover a great range of books and authors, from titles written for younger teens such as Richard Peck's 1990 title *Ghosts I Have Been* (Viking Press, 1977) to Francesca Lia Block's classic *Weetzie Bat* books for older readers honored in 2005. With two new awards, the Odyssey Award, first given in January 2008, and the William C. Morris YA Debut Award, approved by the YALSA Board of Directors and to debut in 2009, it is clear that YALSA continues to play a pivotal role in raising awareness about the expansion in literature and material for young adults. There is no doubt that YALSA's awards are key to spreading the word about the ever-growing range of teen literature.

YALSA's Margaret A. Edwards, Alex, and Michael L. Printz Awards provide a starting point for building knowledge of and appreciation for young adult literature. Written by nationally recognized authorities in providing library services to teenagers, this guidebook brings together essential information about these YALSA awards in one place, clearly making *The Official YALSA Awards Guidebook* a core purchase for libraries. I encourage teachers, librarians, parents, and even teens to use this book as either an introduction to these time-tested award lists or as a resource for expanding your perspective about the wide array of engaging books targeted specifically to teenagers. By learning more about YALSA's awards, every librarian working with teenagers, from generalists to teen specialists, can greatly improve the service they provide teenagers in their libraries. And, in the end, that is the greatest accomplishment of all.

Paula Brehm-Heeger

Preface

Young adult literature is now one of the fastest-growing segments in book publishing and is a highly regarded field of study in its own right. In addition to demographic influences, today's burgeoning interest in this literary segment has been greatly influenced by the Young Adult Library Services Association (YALSA) and its literary awards program. YALSA started bringing attention to young adult literature 20 years ago when it began establishing literary awards for young adult books. The first of these awards, The Margaret A. Edwards Award, given for a writer's lifetime contribution to young adult literature was first given in 1988 to S. E. Hinton. It was soon followed by the Alex Awards, for adult books with particular appeal to teens, in 1998. The third YALSA award was the popular Michael L. Printz Award for excellence in young adult literature, first given in 2000 to Walter Dean Myers. Through these awards, YALSA has educated the public about the growing field of YA literature and furthered twin missions of encouraging reading among young adults and educating the professionals who work with young adults

YALSA now builds on this success by publishing the volume you are now holding in your hands, *The Official YALSA Awards Guidebook*. The Association's members and staff began compiling this guide in order to have a comprehensive, authoritative source of information about its major literary awards so readers, teachers, and librarians could find information about each award and advice about promoting reading of these stellar books in one easy-to-use source. The Association is proud to finally have an official historical summation of the awards, a checklist for collection development, a reader's advisory tool, and a book that interested browsers can use to explore YA literary history, trends, authors, and titles of note.

The timing for this book is propitious. The confluence of several events made it seem that YALSA and young adult literature have now achieved critical mass. Some 2008 marks:

- The fiftieth anniversary of YALSA
- The twentieth anniversary of the Edwards award
- The recent establishment of three new awards: the Odyssey Award for Excellence in Audiobook Production in 2008, a joint award given with

the Association for Library Service to Children and sponsored by Booklist; the William C. Morris Debut YA Award to honor a first-time author
writing for teens in 2009; and the YALSA Award for Excellence in Nonfiction for Young Adults in 2010

- The inaugural Young Adult Literature Symposium sponsored by YALSA
to be held biennially starting in November 2008

All of these events spoke to the need for a comprehensive volume summing up
the YALSA awards to date.

The time was also right for asking the experts involved in the beginnings of
the awards to contribute essays to remind the rest of us how it all started. The
contributors to this volume comprise a who's who of YALSA luminaries and
experts in both literature and services to young adults:

- YALSA Past President Michael Cart writes about the Printz Award.
- Betty Carter, a former YALSA board member who edited the first two
volumes of *Best Books for Young Adults* and served on the inaugural Alex
Awards committee, covers the Alex Awards.
- YALSA Past President Mary Arnold tells us about the Edwards Award.
- RoseMary Honnold, current editor of *Young Adult Library Services*,
YALSA's official journal, shares her knowledge of programming for teens
using the best literature available.
- YALSA Past President Pam Spencer Holley wrote the excellent annota-
tions for each book listed.

This volume was also lucky enough to tap the expertise of two rising stars
who will carry YALSA and the banner of YA lit into the future. Paula Brehm-
Heeger, the 2007–2008 president of YALSA, wrote the foreword to this book.
The chapter on the role award winners can play in effective collection develop-
ment was written by Erin Downey Howerton, who served on the 2008 Edwards
Award selection committee and currently edits YALSA's e-newsletter *YAttitudes*.

All of the people who contributed to this work encourage you to use this
volume actively. Share it with teens who love to read and with teens who don't
know what to read next. Share it with colleagues who want to know more about
young adult literature. Make sure your library has a reference copy, but have a
circulating copy as well. Use your personal copy as a reading log, mark it up with
your own notes and reactions to each title—have a dialogue with this book,
with your colleagues, and with the teens you serve. Young adult literature is a
dynamic field, one that welcomes passion and participation—join the discussion!

Tina Frolund

Acknowledgments

All acknowledgement, praise, and thanks must go to the contributors who truly wrote this book: Pam Spencer Holley, Betty Carter, Michael Cart, RoseMary Honnold, and Mary Arnold. Their knowledge, expertise, and generosity are the reason this volume could be created. Paula Brehm-Heeger and Erin Downey Howerton took time from active careers to contribute their expertise as well.

YALSA's Executive Director Beth Yoke was an early and enthusiastic supporter of this book, and Stephanie Kuenn, Communications Specialist at YALSA, has also been vital to the production of this book.

Part I

Why Award Winners Matter:

Essential Background and Authoritative Advice

Chapter 1

Using Award Winners to Build Better Young Adult Collections

Erin Downey Howerton

Award-winning books will change the shape of your collection forever. More important, they will have a lasting impact on the lives of the teen patrons that you serve. The themes and concepts explored in books that win the Printz, Edwards, Odyssey, and Alex Awards can present challenges as well as opportunities, and we must face both head-on as professionals in the library field and advocates of young adult readers.

Whether you have a long-established YA collection or are just starting a new one, it is well worth your time to review your library's collection policy. If you do not have one, or if youth collections are not mentioned, then you must work with your library's administration to draft an inclusive policy that gives parity to adult and youth materials. Some libraries mandate the inclusion of certain award winners, such as purchasing all the albums that have won a Grammy or making sure that all the National Book Award winners are added to the collection. A similar clause should be added for materials that win prestigious youth media awards. Provisions should be similarly made for challenges—there should be a clearly written and easily understood portion of your collection policy on how to handle potential objections to library materials. It may seem like courting trouble to draft all of these policies out in a time when you are not facing criticism from your patrons, but having well-written policies in place beforehand is crucial to protect the library and your collection from censorship.

If you do not have a separate young adult collection, then your task is a little more challenging. Making sure that teen readers are able to easily identify and borrow media award winners will mean that you provide ample readers' advisory tools both online and off. In the library, you can offer bookmarks and award lists in several formats—draw on your knowledge of your community to make these relevant to your teens. Consider exploring ways to make award-winning books more visible in your library catalog by contacting your tech support team or your vendor for options such as icons or in-catalog lists. Explore the use of physical indicators so that if the books are mixed in with adult or children's collections they can be easily located while you work toward creating a separate collection for YA readers. If you cannot afford to purchase all of the award and honor titles from the Printz, Edwards, Alex, and Odyssey every year, continue to publicize the titles so that teens can be aware of them. Interlibrary loan can supplement your budget, and high usage can even make the case to library administration that the books are popular enough to justify expanding your budget.

A very important consideration must be given to your coworkers. Many librarians do not consider themselves teen-serving librarians, but when young adults approach the desk needing readers' advisory all librarians should have a few reliable favorites to recommend. Assist your fellow librarians by drawing their attention to these award-winning books.

- Share critical reviews and speeches by the award winners with your colleagues. The acceptance speeches by the Printz and Edwards winners are published every year in *Young Adult Library Services*. This resource can help readers connect with the author's writing experience on topics some may consider controversial.
- Share your favorite YA award-winning reads on the staff room bulletin board, start a blog where you record some of your reading and reactions, or periodically send an e-mail with your recent reads. Be sure to talk equally about content as you do about what sort of teen would most appreciate each particular book, and imagine hypothetical situations in which you could help a teen connect with subject matter that is outside their own experience. For example, you might have coworkers claim that suburban Caucasian teens can't relate to the incarcerated African-American teen in Walter Dean Myers' *Monster*. Help the librarians around you to see the value of exposing your young adult patrons to a variety of voices and the full spectrum of human experience. Not every book is for every teen, but these award-winning books can promote empathy and understanding.
- Make sure other youth-serving professionals in your community are aware of the year's winners. YALSA awards are not as long established as other awards, such as the Caldecott and Newbery, and we need to continue to work to promote awareness in our communities so they understand the impact of these books. If the local bookstore is also promoting teen media

award winners, then your library collection can help reinforce the message that these books are worthy of a second look by teen readers. Keep your counterparts in other library settings aware of award winners by offering to booktalk them at staff meetings, professional development days, or informally in other settings. The more readers you have in the community who are conversant with the actual content of award-winning books, the better the chance that they will fall into the hands of young readers who want and need to read them.

When you add YA award-winning books to your collection, you then have an incredible asset—a core go-to list of books that provides both popularity and quality to your teen patrons. One of the first things you should do to enhance the use of this collection is to identify read-alikes for YA award winners both up and down the ability scale. By identifying similar themes and tones you can provide excellent readers' advisory that can serve your patrons well wherever they are in their reading lives. Some younger teens may not yet be ready to handle, say, the treatment of genetic manipulation in Alex Award winner Kazuo Ishiguro's *Never Let Me Go*. It's useful to know books for younger readers with a similar treatment of the theme, like *Star Split* by Kathryn Lasky or, for a reader more fond of modern American settings, *My Sister's Keeper* by Jodi Picoult. Older readers who can't get enough of *Never Let Me Go* may also like other adult titles like the *Beggars in Spain* series by Nancy Kress. When you identify a range of books that center on the award-winning one you help readers step in and out of the reading experience and prolong the thought that they spend on such themes, helping to develop a deeper appreciation and understanding in their reading life.

Different YA award winners also require slightly different treatment in your collection. While every year's Printz and Alex winners are frequently still in hardback issue, the Edwards winners are likely in paperback editions since one of the conditions of the award is that the book(s) being honored have been in print for at least five years or more. Therefore, you should assess any old copies in your collection to see if you need to buy multiple new copies in paperback (which teens persistently indicate as their preferred format for reading). One thing to watch for are old, outdated covers or worn, dirty pages and bindings. It will pay off in increased circulation to spend a few dollars on a new paperback that will circulate among today's teens as compared to an old copy that is showing its age. While you're at it, make sure that older Edwards winners are available to teens in your YA collection. Reading the Edwards Award winners is a sure bet for librarians new to the field to familiarize themselves with YA literature and its development over the years. It's almost a history of YA lit course all on its own!

Similarly, it is sometimes worthwhile to point out the other awards that a YA award winner has garnered. More conservative readers might warm to Edwards winner Chris Crutcher's books once they learn that he has also received the St. Katherine Drexel Award from the Catholic Library Association. Readers who may believe that graphic novels are of dubious merit would benefit from knowing that Printz winner *American Born Chinese* was also a finalist for the National Book Award in the Young People's Literature category. A wide knowledge of the variously recognized merits of award-winning books and their authors can serve as testimony to their impact on readers.

Make sure that your audiobook collection is also up to date—don't forget to watch for audio versions of Printz, Alex, and Edwards Awards books so that you can offer readers a variety of formats in which to enjoy the latest winners. Odyssey Award winners are, of course, selected for their superior audio qualities, and libraries should strive to own these in the formats most used by their patrons, which are increasingly digital. Teen-friendly audio formats include audio CDs, MP3 CDs, downloadable audiobooks, and other emerging formats like the Playaway. If your current vendor or jobber is not carrying these titles in formats your teens want and use, then by all means ask them to start doing so. Raise your concerns so that your patrons' needs are known to the publishing industry.

Remember that while adding YA award-winning books to your collection is important, it is only the first step. Your expertise will help bring these books to life and make them truly available to teen readers. Young adults don't always gravitate to books with shiny medals on them, and books simply sitting on shelves don't always find their own readership without the skills that a prepared librarian can offer. While you may be prepared for the challenges, remember to stay grounded in the opportunities that these books can offer your patrons. With your help, they will continue to find and connect with readers for generations to come.

Chapter 2

Marketing Award-winning Books to Teens

RoseMary Honnold

How do you sell the best of the best to teens? Often the award-winning books are the more challenging reads and are not among the popular series books passed around by teens, so young-adult librarians and school librarians have the task to put these wonderful books into teens', teachers', and parents' hands. Engaging independent programs, intriguing displays, informative handouts, educational curriculum tie-ins, and entertaining promotional commercials during social programs are tools to help you promote great award-winning books.

Display

First-line promotion is an attractive display for the award winners. Create a special shelf or end cap display for Printz, Alex, and Edwards winning titles. Add spine labels and seals to the books to bring attention to the honor these titles have received (available from ALA at www.alastore.ala.org, click on "ALA Award Posters and Seals"). Current title covers can be scanned and posted on a bulletin board or slat wall above the display that so when they are checked out the titles are visible and available for placing holds.

Edwards Award authors can be featured in a display one author at a time. Display a photo of the author, the author's winning books, and a biography or autobiography if one is available. Include a notebook or graffiti poster on which readers can write a note if they have read any of the titles displayed. Add award bookmarks from ALA or create your own with a list of other titles by the author.

Whenever possible, display books with the front cover facing forward so the cover can help sell the book to the reader. If your library discourages labeling books with spine labels or seals, you can still bring notice to these books with your own custom-made bookmarks. Easily created in most word processing or publishing software programs, the bookmark can say "Printz Award" or other award on one end to stick out the top of the book. The remaining part of the bookmark can include interesting quotes from the author, a photo, a summary, or reviews. Make several copies so they can be replaced as needed.

YALSA publishes flyers for the awards ceremonies for the attendees with photos of the authors and interesting biographical information. Slipped into an acrylic sign holder with the author's book standing beside it makes an easy table center or small-space display. Download photos from the Internet or scan author photos from book jackets if you haven't been lucky enough to attend an event to hear these authors speak.

Also available at the YALSA Web site are annotated lists of winning titles. These lists can be helpful to readers, parents, and teachers. Some teachers assign an award winner as a reading project, and a ready-printed list that can be picked up and taken home, to school, or just to the catalog is helpful.

When the winners are announced, make a badge to wear at the library that says "Ask Me About the Printz Award" or "Ask Me About the Edwards Award." Take this opportunity to tell readers some interesting trivia about the awards, like how the titles are chosen and who Michael Printz and Margaret Edwards were.

A slide show for a screensaver on Internet-access computers is a means of reaching those teens who never quite make it to the bookshelves. Create a jpg file with an image of the book cover, an announcement of the award, a picture of the author—just keep it simple enough to read at a glance. Make one for each title for an interesting slide show worth watching.

Play

During the weeks leading up to the awards announcements at the ALA Midwinter Meeting the excitement builds up on the YA librarian discussion lists. Debates, mock votes—everyone voices an opinion about their favorite books of the year. Share this excitement with your teens. You can hold your own mock awards contest and ceremony after the announcements.

As the librarian book discussion lists narrow down the lists of books in the running, you might like to display those titles as teen librarians' favorites and ask teens to vote on them. While we never know for sure which titles are going to be chosen (unless we are on an awards committee), often the discussions cover books that make the final cut.

Do you have teens who love to debate and talk about books? Encourage them to make a case for their favorite books by creating commercials to present at programs and book discussions and in classrooms. Then hold a vote to see who made the best case for their title. Who convinced the most teens that their book was the one to read?

A "Battle of the Awards Books" competition among teams from different classrooms or even different schools can attract attention to these titles. A fun approach is using a PowerPoint, Jeopardy-style trivia game. Choose a winning title for each column and five questions about each title. Other versions might have five questions about the awards or the authors. Play in the same way as the Jeopardy television show, with individual players or in teams, like high school quiz team competitions. Project the game onto a big screen and add images and sounds or music to the program to make it even more fun for the audience and players. A model for a Jeopardy PowerPoint game is available at www.cplrmh .com/JeopardyGames.html. An example PowerPoint game about the Margaret Edwards Awards is available here: www.ala.org/yalsa/edwards.

Give the readers in your library clubs an awards challenge. Provide a reading journal for all the titles of one of the awards or all the winners of a year. At the end of the year, throw a party for the participants and award a special prize to those who complete their reading journals. Paperback copies of past winners are great ideas for prizes for summer reading programs or for Teen Read Week giveaways.

You can also create quizzes to hand out at programs. Match first lines and titles, match titles to awards, or create a word find of titles or authors or a cross-word of titles and authors. Word finds and crosswords can be created at www.puzzlemaker.com. Place a stack of these puzzles by the book display. You can offer a prize for completing the puzzle.

Read

Have you had mixed success with teen book discussion groups? A fresh approach may be to recharge your group. Make it your group's assignment to read and vote on the award winners ALA award committee style. Teens in your book clubs will enjoy hearing inside information about the authors and books. Share what you learn at conferences or by creating interesting Web sites about the authors.

Pass It On is an activity you can use in your teen group to introduce new books or award books. Collect at least one title for every teen and pass them out. Tell them a few tips on how to review a book quickly: Read the covers and the blurbs, a few lines in the book, and look at any illustrations to determine the sex and age of the main character, the setting, and the basic plot. Give the teens about three minutes to look over their books and ask them to pass their title to the left. Repeat the review process. Do this one more time and begin discussion. Ask the teens to tell the title and author of the book they are holding and anything else they would like to tell about it. The other two teens who reviewed the book are to chime in with comments, including whether they would read the book and what kind of reader might enjoy the book. After these discussions, many of the books will usually be checked out.

Booktalk award winners to classrooms and at library club meetings. Try reading aloud the first chapter of an award winner to your teens at your next Teen Advisory Board meeting. Take several titles with you and let the teens choose which ones you should booktalk. Experienced and new booktalkers find it helpful to tape the booktalk notes to the back of the book so the front cover can be shown when sharing the book. When an award winner is of a specific genre, be sure to share it with teens and teachers who would be interested.

Passages of winning titles can be reworked for readers' theater presentations. Readers' theater is performed with few, if any, props and there is no memorization for the players. The parts are read, but practice makes delivery more interesting to the audience. For a bit of fun, a simple readers' theater reading can be done on the fly in the classroom or at a meeting by giving each player a line or two and numbering them so they are read in order. For content, select a passage of dialogue in the book or write a commercial for the book. Teens can help with either of these approaches. Be careful not to reveal any plot secrets that only a reader should get to know. The purpose is for the teens to sell the book to other teen readers, like a booktalk, but more fun!

Show

Award-winning books can make great storylines for movie scripts. A movie license is required to show films in the library. Two popular companies are Moving Licensing USA at www.movlic.com/library/library.html and Motion Picture Licensing Corporation at www.mplc.com. License fees for libraries are usually based on the number of active patrons.

Movie Licensing USA is a licensing agent for Walt Disney Pictures, Touchstone Pictures, Hollywood Pictures, Warner Bros., Columbia Pictures, TriStar Pictures, Paramount Pictures, DreamWorks Pictures, Metro-Goldwyn-Mayer, Universal Pictures, Sony Pictures, United Artists, and various independent studios, and provides the Movie Copyright Compliance Site License. Send an e-mail to Mail@movlic.com to inquire about cost. There are separate telephone numbers for schools and public libraries. For Movie Licensing USA for schools, call 877-321-1300 (toll-free). For Movie Licensing USA for public libraries, call 888-267-2658 (toll-free).

Motion Picture Licensing represents more than 60 producers and distributors, including Walt Disney Pictures, Warner Bros., Scholastic Entertainment, McGraw-Hill, Sony Pictures Classics, Tommy Nelson, and World Almanac, and provides an Umbrella License. Call 800-462-8855 or send an e-mail to info@mplc.com.

Programs that promote reading the book and seeing the movie can lead to interesting discussions on the difference and similarities of the book and the movie. Does an award-winning book necessarily mean an award-winning movie? Even if a movie isn't available or forthcoming, it is fun to discuss what actors the teens would cast as the major characters.

An established teen group in your library will enjoy a field trip to see a movie in the theater and have a lot of fun discussing the movie compared to the book over pizza afterward. Friends of the Library groups will often sponsor a movie and pizza party for your teens.

Learn

Award winners can be promoted in the classroom with a "Battle of the Awards Books." The teacher can assign several award-winning titles for the students to read. Depending on the size of the class and the number of books, at least one reader of each book should be on each team. The teams then compete with one another in a trivia contest about the books. The contest can be held in elimination rounds and the winners can challenge another classroom. Questions should include main character, setting, and key plot elements, and tiebreakers can be questions about the authors.

While many of the award winners are selected for literary merit and would be suitable for any English class discussion, several titles will support other subject areas and should be brought to the teachers' attention. Teachers also need to be aware of any issues in the book that might limit its appeal to certain audiences. For example, strong language, violence, or sexual content may preclude some titles from being used in a middle school or junior high classroom setting. Your knowledge of young adult literature will be more valuable to the school if you are sensitive to their parameters. Here are a few examples of possible curriculum connections:

Social Studies

- Yang, Gene Luen. 2006. *American Born Chinese*. New York: First Second. Printz Award winner about Chinese Americans.
- Stratton, Allan. 2004. *Chanda's Secrets*. Toronto: Annick Press. Printz Honor book about AIDS in Africa.
- Bates, Judy Fong. 2005. *Midnight at the Dragon Café*. New York: Counterpoint. Alex Award about Chinese immigrants who moved to Ontario.
- Meyers, Kent. 2004. *Work of Wolves*. Orlando, FL: Harcourt. Alex Award winner about Native American suspense.

History

- Schmidt, Gary D. 2004. *Lizzie Bright and the Buckminster Boy*. New York: Clarion Books. Printz Honor book about race relations in 1911 along the Maine coast.
- Anderson, M. T. 2006. *The Astonishing Life of Octavian Nothing, Traitor to the Nation: The Pox Party*. Cambridge, MA: Candlewick Press. Printz Honor Book about race experiments during the Revolutionary War.
- Zusak, Markus. 2006. *The Book Thief.* New York: Alfred A. Knopf. Printz Honor book about the Holocaust.
- Donnelly, Jennifer. 2003. *A Northern Light*. San Diego: Harcourt. Printz Honor book about a murder in the Adirondacks in 1906, based on a true story.
- Chambers, Aidan. 2002. *Postcards from No Man's Land*. New York: Dutton Children's Books. Printz Award winner about WWII.
- Kurson, Robert. 2004. *Shadow Divers: The True Adventure of Two Americans Who Risked Everything to Solve One of the Last Mysteries of World War II*. New York: Random House. Alex Award winner about discovering the secrets of a sunken U boat from WWII.
- Doig, Ivan. 2006. *The Whistling Season*. Orlando, FL: Harcourt. Alex Award winner about life in Montana in the early 1900s.
- Hamamura, John. 2006. *Color of the Sea*. New York: Thomas Dunne Books. Alex Award winner about the Japanese American experience though WWII.

Write

As a classroom writing assignment or a writer's club activity, teen writers may try writing alternative endings for the novels, or writing fan fiction using the same characters, or creating acrostic poems from titles. Create a newspaper or newsletter about a book with headlines and stories featuring characters and events from a book and explanation about the award it has won.

Author Author!

Invite an award-winning author to your libraries or schools. A cooperative venture may make this sometimes expensive event possible. Partnerships between public schools and public libraries will divide the transportation expense to bring an author to the area. Assign teen reporters to interview the authors when they visit and share the interviews in the local newspaper, library newsletter, and online with links to the author's Web sites. Recorded interviews may be used in a podcast with permission from the author.

Art Projects

Encourage the cartoonist within by asking your anime/manga club to create a comic strip mural of the major events in an award-winning novel. Sponsor an art contest for teen artists to create movie posters for the novels, featuring the actors they would like to see play the characters. Teens may enjoy creating new book cover art to frame and hang in the YA area.

Bookmobiles can add another dimension to your YA room décor. Scan, cut out, and laminate book covers, author pictures, award medals, or use the ALA seals. String with fishing line and attach to a dowel to create a mobile to hang from the ceiling.

Internet Projects

The Internet is a great tool for promoting reading and books to teens because they love being online. Here are several ideas for promoting award books online:

- Podcast booktalks by teens on the library's teen Web site or blog.
- Annotate a title on your blog and provide a link to the award, to the catalog to reserve, and to the author page.
- Get connected with your teen readers on sites like www.goodreads.com, a social networking site for readers. Readers share what they read, give ratings and reviews, and connect with more readers.
- Participate in online chats with authors.
- Have some real fans? Take pictures of the teens with the books and send a group fan mail to the author.

There are many fun, interesting, and educational approaches to connecting teens with award-winning books. I hope some of these ideas in this chapter will spark your imagination. Ask your teens for feedback and participation and you can't go wrong!

Part II
The Awards

Chapter 3

The Alex Award

Introductory Overview

Betty Carter

In 1994, at a Young Adult Library Services Association (YALSA) preconference in Miami, respected editor Richard Jackson shocked participants with five little words that defined the publishing industry's policy at that time: "Young adult now ends at fourteen." Talk about a wake-up call. This one was as insistent as any alarm clock, sounding an unwanted signal that books published in young adult houses would target younger teens and neglect older ones. Librarians interested in young adults and their reading pushed no snooze buttons—they sat up and took action. One of those actions led them to "fall back" with a kind of professional daylight savings that returned them to the early days of young adult librarianship and literature.

The most enduring voice from that past comes from Margaret Alexander Edwards, called Alex by her friends and the patron saint of young adult librarianship by her colleagues. Edwards spent her entire career, from 1932 to 1962, at the Enoch Pratt Free Library in Baltimore, but her work in establishing young adult collections and readers advisory spread throughout the nation, particularly with her collection of essays *The Fair Garden and the Swarm of Beasts*, first published in 1969. She believed that young adult librarians should "take each individual, whatever his reading level, and develop him to his full potential as a reader, widening his interests and deepening his understanding until he came to know that he was a member of one race—the human race—and a citizen of one planet—the earth" (Edwards, 2002, p. 68). This development, in Edwards's mind, came through wide reading, and this reading should allow a young adult to move into adult books as soon as he or she were ready, "showing him [the teenager] how to develop critical ability, how to distinguish between sham and truth in writing, how to become acquainted with the great literary heritage that is his, so that when he finishes high school he will be already on the way to broadening his limited experience and enriching his understanding through adult books" (Edwards, 2002, pp. 56–57).

Hollywood likes Alex winners!

Big budget films have been made from:

The Time Traveler's Wife (2008)
The Kite Runner (2007)
Stardust (2007) with Michelle Pfeiffer, Claire Danes, and Robert De Niro
Flags of Our Fathers (2006) directed by Clint Eastwood
Shackleton (2002) with Kenneth Brannagh. Ernest Shackleton's voyage is also the subject of the documentary called *The Endurance* (2000) that incorporates footage and still photographs from the actual expedition.
The Perfect Storm (2000) starring George Clooney, John C. Reilly, and Diane Lane

Look also for filmed versions of *Into Thin Air: Death on Everest* (1997), *Snow in August* (2001), *Girl with a Pearl Earring* (2003), *Plainsong* (2004), and *The Dive from Clausen's Pier* (2005).

In 1988 Edwards died, but her influence continues through the work of those she mentored, through her writing, and through her estate. As she writes in her will: "since I have faith in young people and am concerned that they read—not only for their personal enjoyment and enrichment but so that they may equip themselves to remake society—I bequeath the bulk of my estate to further the personal reading of young adults" (Margaret Alexander Trust, 1991).

With that background in mind, fast-forward your professional clocks to 1997. Deb Taylor, former YALSA president and coordinator of school and student services at Enoch Pratt Free Library, spearheaded a grant from the Edwards trustees to fund, for five years, The Adult Books for Young Adults Project, an undertaking that would highlight the role of adult books in young adults' reading lives, making it "possible to expand programs bringing young adults and their literature together in a way that is consonant with Edwards's pioneering interests" (American Library Association, 1997). The ad hoc committee created with that charge, of which I was privileged to be a member, decided to have five consecutive programs at the American Library Association's (ALA's) convention that would focus on the role of adult books in young adult reading and to explore the possibility of creating an award for adult books that spoke to young adults.

British author Neil Gaiman has won two Alex awards: for *Anansi Boys* in 2006 and for *Stardust* in 2000.

This ad hoc committee's initial meeting occurred during 1997's ALA Annual Conference and the members decided to (1) create a list of ten adult books published during the current year that held great promise for young adults and (2) to use those books as a springboard for the initial conference program at the ALA Annual Conference in 1998. I honestly don't remember how we came up with the number ten for books that would be recognized—perhaps all of us watched way too much David Letterman—but I believe the rationale behind the decision (which stands today) was that this number gave the latitude to explore and identify many areas of adult publishing that might be of potential interest and value for young adults.

Once the committee decided to create the list, or the Alex Awards, *Booklist* editor Bill Ott offered both financial and professional backing for the venture. (Both the Alex Awards and the *Booklist* affiliation were approved by the YALSA board as a permanent institution in 2002.) Generous and natural, this partnership creates a logical progression from the thoughtful acknowledgment *Booklist* gives to adult books for young adults by indicating in repeat notes those adult titles of general interest to young adults, those of limited interest, and those with strong curricula connections, to recognizing those books of greatest distinction. In the early years of the award, *Booklist* additionally allotted valuable page space to announce the Alex winners during National Library Week.

There has never been any attempt to balance the list, to have, for example, a range of genres, sophistication, and targeted age levels, but a list with ten books can approach that kind of variety. And over the years, it has. As an interesting aside, the original task force operated under a mandate to address diversity in literature, but Deb Taylor never shared that piece of information with the group. She believed in the integrity of the ad hoc committee, that the committee would examine books, that they would select the strongest books, and that those choices would naturally reflect the diversity of the publishing industry. Her decision proved both right and wise.

> If you like to read nonfiction, Alex is the award for you. Every year several nonfiction titles are included among the Alex winners. Subjects as diverse as the rats that inhabit New York City (*Rats: Observations on the History and Habitat of the City's Most Unwanted Inhabitants*, Alex 2005), the human body—alive (*The Secret Family: Twenty-Four Hours Inside the Mysterious Worlds of Our Minds and Bodies*, Alex 1998) and dead (*Stiff*, Alex 2004), growing up in poverty (*The Glass Castle: A Memoir*, Alex 2006), and first jobs (*Educating Esme*, Alex 2000) have been covered.

Capping each list to ten books allows the committee to winnow out the less than sterling adult books that teenagers read. It's important to remember that just because a book is published in an adult house does not mean it is necessarily fine literature or the kind of book that might lead a teenager to the lofty goals Margaret Edwards believed reading held. On the other hand, the Alex list never intended to be a short list of books for the college bound. There are books that may speak more directly to the younger adolescent (such as Mel Odom's [2001] *The Rover*) or even to the reluctant reader (*Lest We Forget: The Passage from Africa to Slavery and Emancipation* [Thomas, 1997], for example). When the original task force decided to create this list of adult books, Deb Taylor told the task force quite clearly what kinds of books we were looking for: "the next *To Kill a Mockingbird* [Lee, 1960]."

Although the winners from the first ten years don't have Harper Lee quaking in her boots, the committees came danged close with many of their choices. In today's world of in-print/out-of-print, 77 of the first 100 Alex winners remain in print as of this writing. This status speaks volumes about the books' endurance throughout the years.

There's an old story that circulates in the south about a young woman preparing her first holiday dinner. She remembered that when her mother cooked the ham, she always chopped off the end of it before putting it in a baking dish. So the daughter followed suit. One year Mama came to dinner and asked her daughter: "What fool thing are you doing by cutting off that good ham?" Her daughter replied, "That's the way you always did it." And Mama replied, "That's just because my baking dish was too small." The point is, that one of the practices of the original task force, born out of convenience, took eight years to change. Remember that the first Alex list was conceived in the summer without a nomination or a single book discussion. At that point the committee decided to discuss nominations during the 1998 Midwinter Meeting and announce the titles during National Library Week, allowing a couple of extra months for reading and deliberations. That pattern continued, but in 2006 it changed with the announcement of the Alex Awards coinciding with all the other ALA book award announcements on Monday morning during the ALA Midwinter Meeting. Such timing is appropriate and lends additional visibility to the awards.

> Look for three graphic novels among the Alex books: *Essex County Volume I: Tales from the Farm* by Jeff Lemire (Alex 2008), *Persepolis* by Marjane Satrapi (Alex 2004), and *One Hundred Demons* by Lynda Barry (Alex 2003).

In addition, the charge to the Adult Books for Young Adults task force to present an annual program focusing on adult books for young adults has been removed from the present Alex Committee. Again, another wise move, for the task force found the dual focus daunting. Not only were we selecting books, but the committee was also creating ways to highlight them. Still, the programs, which usually involved a small introduction to both Edwards and the importance of adult books in the reading lives of young adults and brief booktalks about each entry on the current list, proved popular over the years, and the Alex committee often chooses to offer a program on each year's winners at the annual conference. The only written record of these programs is the initial keynote address from 1998, "Back to the Future with Adult Books for the Teenage Reader" by Richard F. Abrahamson, which was reprinted in the *Journal of Youth Services* and the Centennial Edition of *The Fair Garden and the Swarm of Beasts*.

What is it about the cold?

The following Alex winners are true stories of heroism under extreme circumstances:

Into Thin Air: A Personal Account of the Mt. Everest Disaster (Alex 1998)
The Perfect Storm: A True Story of Men Against the Sea (Alex 1998)
The Endurance: Shackleton's Legendary Antarctic Expedition (Alex 1999)
High Exposure: An Enduring Passion for Everest and Unforgiving Places (Alex 2000)
The Hungry Ocean: A Swordboat Captain's Journey (Alex 2000)
In the Heart of the Sea: The Tragedy of the Whaleship Essex (Alex 2001)
Shadow Divers: The True Adventures of Two Americans Who Risked Everything to Solve One of the Last Mysteries of World War II (Alex 2005)
Swimming to Antarctica: Tales of a Long Distance Swimmer (Alex 2005)

And for one more story about the cold, read *Antarctica* (Alex 1999), Kim Stanley Robinson's fictional account of the clash of interests over the slowly melting Antarctic.

Other challenges the initial task force faced remain the same. The most daunting task is simply finding the books for consideration. Where does one start when faced with the entire output of adult publishing? The first stop is generally with the journals, the repeat notes in *Booklist* and the "Adult Books for Young Adults" column in *School Library Journal*, for example. But, don't ignore nontraditional sources, such as those heavy on popular culture like *Entertainment Weekly* and *People*. In addition, the initial ad hoc committee (and it appears the succeeding ones as well) paid close attention to first novels (*Peace Like a River* [Enger, 2000] or *The Dive from Clausen's Pier* [Packer, 2002]), memoirs (*Caucasia* [Senna, 1998] and *The Glass Castle* [Walls, 2006]), authors known for previous appeal (such as Pat Conroy [2001] for *My Losing Season*), accounts of high adventure (*The Perfect Storm* [Junger, 1999] or *Into Thin Air* [Krakauer, 1997]), and topics such as those first years after high school (*Getting In* [Boylan, 1998] and *An American Insurrection: The Battle of Oxford, Mississippi* [Doyle, 2001]), the world of work (*Nickel and Dimed* [Ehrenreich, 2001] and *Educating Esme* [Coddell, 1999]), or scientific accounts (*The Secret Family* [Bodanis, 1997] or *Seeing In the Dark* [Ferris, 2001]) not traditionally covered in young adult literature. One point that underscores the uniqueness of this finding and deciding on titles is that of the one hundred present Alex Award winners, only 24 titles, or approximately one-quarter of the total books, appeared on corresponding Best Books for Young Adults lists.

After creating a consideration list, committees must ask themselves two questions: (1) what is the potential appeal to young adults? and (2) what are the components of this book that make it an award winner? Although committee choices are by nature defined by what a particular group believes at one particular point in time, other indications, such as the subsequent young adult abridgements of *Flags of Our Fathers* (Bradley and Powers, 2000) and *In the Heart of the Sea* (Philbrick, 2000), or critical acclaim for books such as *Plainsong* (Haruf, 1999), indicate that others also asked at least one of the two questions and came up with similar conclusions. Still, the Alex Awards recognize a unique list of titles that hold the potential of meeting many needs, some known and some unknown, of teenage readers.

Sports is another area of interest for Alex awards. Sports fans will want to read:

Blind Side: Evolution of a Game (Alex 2007)
Counting Coup: A True Story of Basketball and Honor on the Little Big Horn (Alex 2001)
Eagle Blue: A Team, a Tribe and a High School Basketball Season in Arctic Alaska (Alex 2007)
My Losing Season (Alex 2003)
Swimming to Antarctica: Tales of a Long-Distance Swimmer (Alex 2005)

When the Adult Books for Young Adults task force began, it filled a void in literature available for young adults. Since, and even during, that time period, young adult publishing has gradually become more sophisticated, reaching quite nicely that older age group; the difference between adult books and young adult books has become more fluid. One Alex winner, Mark Haddon's (2004) *The Curious Incident of the Dog in the Night-time*, was originally published in Great Britain as a young adult book, and Marcus Zusak's (2007) *The Book Thief*, a young adult publication in America, was originally published adult in Australia. Harry Potter has as many adult fans as juvenile ones, while *The Astonishing Life of Octavian Nothing, Traitor to the Nation, Volume 1: The Pox Party* (Anderson, 2006), as well as other young adult publications, rivals many adult books for sheer elegance in writing. But Alex winners put more books on the table for librarians to read and use for readers advisory. And that's what Margaret Edwards was about: wide reading and solid recommending in order to create lifetime readers of thousands of young adults. The Alex Awards mirror her mission.

References

Abrahamson, Richard F. 1998. "Back to the Future with Adult Books for the Teenage Reader." *Journal of Youth Services in Libraries* 11 (summer): 378–387.

American Library Association. 1997. "YALSA receives $25,000 grant from the Margaret Alexander Trust" [press release]. Chicago: American Library Association.

Anderson, M. T. 2006. *The Astonishing Case of Octavia Nothing, Traitor to the Nation*, vol. 1. Cambridge, UK: Candlewick.

Bodanis, David. 1997. *The Secret Family: Twenty-four Hours Inside the Mysterious Worlds of our Minds and Bodies.* New York: Simon & Schuster.

Boylan, James Finney. 1998. *Getting In.* New York: Warner.

Bradley, James and Ron Powers. 2000. *Flags of our Fathers.* New York: Bantam.

Coddell, Esme. 1999. *Educating Esme.* Chapel Hill: Algonquin.

Conroy, Pat. 2001. *My Losing Season.* New York: Doubleday/Nan A. Talese.

Doyle, William. 2001. *An American Insurrection: The Battle of Oxford, Mississippi, 1962.* New York: Doubleday.

Edwards, Margaret A. 2002. *The Fair Garden and the Swarm of Beasts: The Library and the Young Adult*, Centennial Edition. Chicago: The American Library Association.

Ehrenreich, Barbara. 2001. *Nickel and Dimed: On (Not) Getting by in Boom-time America.* New York: Holt/Metropolitan.

Enger, Keith. 2000. *Peace Like a River.* New York: Atlantic Monthly.

Ferris, Timothy. 2001. *Seeing in the Dark: How Backyard Stargazers are Probing Deep Space and Guarding Earth from Interplanetary Peril.* New York: Simon & Schuster.

Haddon, Mark. 2004. *The Curious Incident of the Dog in the Night-time.* New York: Doubleday.

Haruf, Kent. 1999. *Plainsong.* New York: Knopf.

Junger, Sebastian. 1999. *The Perfect Storm: A True Story of Men Against the Sea.* New York: Norton.

Krakauer, Jon. 1997. *Into Thin Air: A Personal Account of the Mt. Everest Disaster.* New York: Villard.

Lee, Harper. 1960. *To Kill a Mockingbird.* Philadelphia: Lippincott.

Margaret Alexander Trust. 1991. *Margaret Alexander Edwards Trust: The Lady, the Librarian, and Her Legacy* [brochure]. Baltimore: Margaret Alexander Trust.

Odom, Mel. 2001. *The Rover.* New York: Tor.

Packer, Ann. 2002. *The Dive from Clausen's Pier.* New York: Knopf.

Philbrick, Nathaniel. 2000. *In the Heart of the Sea: The Tragedy of the Whaleship Essex.* New York: Viking.

Senna, Danzy. 1998. *Caucasia.* New York: Putnam/Riverhead.

Thomas, Velma Marie. 1997. *Lest We Forget: The Passage from Africa to Slavery and Emancipation.* New York: Crown.

Walls, Jeannette. 2006. *The Glass Castle.* New York: Scribner.

Zuzak, Marcus. 2007. *The Book Thief.* New York: Knopf.

The Alex Winners: An Annotated Bibliography

Pam Spencer Holley

2008 Winners

BEAH, ISHMAEL. *A Long Way Gone: Memoirs of a Boy Soldier*. Farrar, Straus & Giroux/Sarah Crichton Books. **NF**
   Beah tells, in his own words, his harrowing experiences as a child soldier in the Sierra Leone civil war.
Subjects: Sierra Leone, Personal Narrative, Child Soldiers

IGUULDEN, CONN. *Genghis: Birth of an Empire*. Delacorte.
   Temujin, the abandoned son of a khan, survives the harsh Asian tundra to become one of the world's greatest military leaders in this absorbing historical tale.
Subjects: Historical Fiction, Mongols, Biographical Fiction, Kings and Rulers

JONES, LLOYD. *Mister Pip*. Random/Dial Press.
   On a war-torn Pacific island, 13-year-old Matilda describes how an eccentric white teacher fires the imaginations of the village children by reading *Great Expectations* aloud.
Subjects: Bouganville Island, Storytelling, Books and Reading

KYLE, ARYN. *The God of Animals*. Scribner.
   After her older sister elopes, 12-year-old Alice is left behind on the family's rundown Colorado horse farm to cope with her distant parents and the unsolved murder of a classmate.
Subjects: Ranches, Colorado, Bildungsromans

LEMIRE, JEFF. *Essex County Volume 1: Tales from the Farm*. Top Shelf Publications.
   In this stark, moving graphic novel, Lester, a recently orphaned ten-year-old, finds escape in a private fantasy world of aliens and superheroes with his friend, a former hockey player.
Subjects: Graphic Novels, Orphans, Friendship

LUTZ, LISA. *The Spellman Files*. Simon & Schuster.
   Isabel can't quit her private investigator job; she works for her family, and they'll kill her if she tries to leave. A quickly paced, quirky mystery.
Subjects: Private Investigators

MALTMAN, THOMAS. *The Night Birds*. Soho.
   Asa, a Minnesota boy growing up in the nineteenth century, learns secrets about his family's violent, complicated past following the bloody Dakota Conflict of 1862.
Subjects: Teenage Boys, Dakota Indians, Minnesota

POLLY, MATTHEW. *American Shaolin: Flying Kicks, Buddhist Monks, and the Legend of Iron Crotch: An Odyssey in the New China*. Penguin/Gotham Books. **NF**
A college student tells his fascinating, funny story about traveling from Kansas to China's Shaolin Temple, where he attempts to master kung fu and find courage.
Subjects: Martial Arts, China, Shao Lin Si

ROTHFUSS, PATRICK. *The Name of the Wind*. DAW.
Homeless thief Kvothe wins a place at the school of magic, where he hopes to learn more about the mysterious Chandrian who murdered his parents.
Subjects: Magicians, Magic, Fantasy

RUFF, MATT. *Bad Monkeys*. HarperCollins
Jane Charlotte earns her living by killing bad people for good reasons in this high-octane, clever thriller of conspiracies, revenge, and secret government agencies.
Subjects: Secret Societies, Vigilantes, Suspense

2007 Winners

CONNOLLY, JOHN. *The Book of Lost Things*. Atria Books.
Lost in a world filled with characters from his beloved fairy and folk tales, loner David is told to find and use *The Book of Lost Things* if he wishes to return home.
Subjects: Fantasy, Fairy Tales, England

DOIG, IVAN. *The Whistling Season*. Harcourt.
Arriving in Montana in the early 1900s to be a housekeeper for three motherless boys, Rose has such winning ways that no one minds her inability to cook.
Subjects: Historical Fiction, Brothers and Sisters, Teachers, Housekeepers, Montana

D'ORSO, MICHAEL. *Eagle Blue: A Team, a Tribe and a High School Basketball Season in Arctic Alaska*. Bloomsbury. **NF**
Living eight miles above the Arctic Circle doesn't diminish the basketball mania that sweeps over Fort Yukon, where almost half of the school population plays to win during the long, cold season of 2004–2005.
Subjects: Sports, Basketball, Native Americans, Gwich'in Tribe, Arctic Circle, Alaska

GRUEN, SARA. *Water for Elephants*. Algonquin Books.
Amid the sequins and spangles of early twentieth-century circus life, Jacob Jankowski's training as a veterinarian helps him survive working for the second-rate Benzini Brothers Spectacular Show on Earth.
Subjects: Historical Fiction, Depression (1929), Circus, Elephants

HAMAMURA, JOHN. *Color of the Sea*. Thomas Dunne Books.
Japanese-Americans Sam and Yanagi have strong family and cultural ties to Japan, ties that are sorely tested after the bombing of Pearl Harbor.
Subjects: Historical Fiction, World War II, Hiroshima, Japanese Americans

JOERN, PAMELA CARTER. *The Floor of the Sky*. University of Nebraska Press.
Toby's pregnant granddaughter Lila joins her in the family's Nebraska Sand Hills home at a perfect time to keep intact the family traditions that bolster their love for the land.
Subjects: Grandmothers, Teen Pregnancy, Nebraska

LEWIS, MICHAEL. *The Blind Side: Evolution of a Game*. Norton. **NF**
Taken off the streets of Memphis, Tennessee, homeless Michael Oher is given love and an education by a wealthy family and now protects the blind side of the quarterback as a left tackle for Ole Miss.
Subjects: Sports, Football, Mississippi

MITCHELL, DAVID. *Black Swan Green*. Random House.
In a month-by-month chronicle, Jason relates his difficult year at school as he contends with stammering, bullies, and the fear of being caught writing poetry for the parish magazine.
Subjects: High School, England

RASH, RON. *The World Made Straight*. H. Holt and Co.
A mutual interest in the Civil War and marijuana draws together former teacher Leonard Shuler and high school dropout Travis Shelton.
Subjects: Marijuana, Civil War Buffs, Male Friendship, South Carolina

SETTERFIELD, DIANE. *The Thirteenth Tale*. Atria Books.
Hired to write the biography of a reclusive author who perpetually lies about her life, Margaret is unprepared for the secrets that Vida de Winter reveals to complete the "thirteenth tale."
Subjects: Authors, Friendship, Secrets, England

2006 Winners

BATES, JUDY FONG. *Midnight at the Dragon Café*. Counterpoint.
Settling into life in a remote Canadian town after fleeing Communist China, Su-Jen witnesses her mother's unhappiness with her elderly father.
Subjects: Ontario, Chinese Canadians

BUCKHANON, KALISHA. *Upstate*. St. Martin's Press.
Separated when 16-year-old Antonio is sent to prison for killing his father, years of his correspondence with Natasha helps both teens prepare for the future, with or without each other.
Subjects: Prison, New York, Imprisoned Teens, African Americans

GAIMAN, NEIL. *Anansi Boys*. William Morrow.
The death of Fat Charlie's father leads to an unexpected meeting with Spider, a brother he didn't know he had and soon doesn't want.
Subjects: Fathers and Sons, Brothers, England

GALLOWAY, GREGORY. *As Simple As Snow*. Putnam.
A nondescript high school sophomore is pursued by new student, Goth girl Anna, whose love of codes, ciphers, and puzzles may contain clues to her unexpected disappearance.
Subjects: High School, Missing Persons, Mystery

ISHIGURO, KAZUO. *Never Let Me Go*. Alfred A. Knopf.
Brought up privileged at Hailsham boarding school, Kathy, Ruth, and Tommy are surprisingly complacent about the roles they'll be assigned as cloned adults.
Subjects: Human Cloning, Organ Donors, England

MARTINEZ, A. LEE. *Gil's All Fright Diner*. Tor.
Running out of gas, vampire Earl and werewolf Duke stop at a small diner in the desert where they're immediately hired to keep zombies from attacking the greasy spoon.
Subjects: Fantasy, Zombies, Vampires, Werewolves

PALWICK, SUSAN. *The Necessary Beggar*. Tor.
Accused of murdering a holy beggar with whom he was in love, Darroti and his family are exiled from their peaceful home to a refugee camp in distant Nevada.
Subjects: Fantasy, Exiles

RAWLES, NANCY. *My Jim*. Crown.
Though each has dreamed of freedom from slavery, when his wife Sadie is sold to a new master, Jim takes off down river with Huck Finn.
Subjects: Slavery, African Americans, Family, Historical Fiction

SCHEERES, JULIA. *Jesus Land: A Memoir*. Counterpoint. **NF**
Scheere's unflinching memoir chronicles life in rural Indiana with her disciplinarian father, fundamentalist mother, and two adopted African-American brothers.
Subjects: Memoir, Family, Interracial Family, Indiana, Dominican Republic, Christianity, Fundamentalism

WALLS, JEANNETTE. *The Glass Castle: A Memoir*. Scribner. **NF**
Raised by two eccentric parents, Walls continues to love them even after watching her mother root through a dumpster and overhearing her father try to pimp her at a bar.
Subjects: Memoir, Family, Poverty, Homelessness, Children of Alcoholics

2005 Winners

ALMOND, STEVE. *Candyfreak: A Journey Through the Chocolate Underbelly of America*. Algonquin Books. **NF**
    This obsessed chocoholic takes the reader on a tour of the best kept secrets in America—little chocolate factories that produce Nashville's Goo Goo Clusters, Philadelphia's Peanut Chews, and Boise's Idaho Spuds.
    Subjects: Candy, Chocolate, Humor

COX, LYNN. *Swimming to Antarctica: Tales of a Long-Distance Swimmer*. Knopf. **NF**
    A noted long-distance ocean swimmer, Cox musters her physical strength and endurance as she becomes the first woman to swim across the frigid waters of the Bering Strait.
    Subjects: Sports, Swimming, Antarctica

HALPIN, BRENDAN. *Donorboy*. Random House/Villard.
    When her lesbian mothers are killed in an accident, 14-year-old Rosaline finds herself living with her biological father, a geeky guy who never expected to be a parent.
    Subjects: Family, Fathers and Daughters

KURSON, ROBERT. *Shadow Divers: The True Adventures of Two Americans Who Risked Everything to Solve One of the Last Mysteries of World War II*. Random House. **NF**
    Discovering a long-forgotten World War II German U-boat off the New Jersey coast inspires two deep-sea divers to locate information about the vessel and its crew.
    Subjects: Shipwrecks, Diving, World War II, U-boats, Adventure

MEYERS, KENT. *Work of Wolves*. Harcourt.
    Three misfits, a horse trainer, German exchange student, and Lakota teen, unite to steal three starving horses from a wealthy, land-obsessed neighbor.
    Subjects: Horses, Ranching, South Dakota

PATCHETT, ANN. *Truth & Beauty: A Friendship*. HarperCollins. **NF**
    Author Patchett tells of her friendship with daredevil Lucy Grealey, author of *Autobiography of a Face*, that lasts until Grealey's death from the childhood cancer that disfigures her face.
    Subjects: Friendship, Disfigurement

PICOULT, JODI. *My Sister's Keeper*. Atria.
    Conceived to provide organs and other help for her critically ill sister, Anna eventually sues her parents to gain the rights to her own body.
    Subjects: Family, Sisters, Mothers and Daughters, Organ Donors, Leukemia

REED, KIT. *Thinner Than Thou*. Tor.

In the near future, Americans are obsessed with their bodies and turn from worshipping God in church to worshiping their shapes in spas run by "reverends."

Subjects: Body Image, Dystopia

SHEPARD, JIM. *Project X*. Knopf.

Tired of the bullying he endures at school, eighth-grader Edwin and his friend Flake concoct a vengeful plan of retaliation.

Subjects: Friendship, School Violence, Revenge

SULLIVAN, ROBERT. *Rats: Observations on the History and Habitat of the City's Most Unwanted Inhabitants*. Bloomsbury. **NF**

Writing as both naturalist and historian, Sullivan's observation of rats in the alleys of New York City leads to an examination of the role these rodents played in the history of the city.

Subjects: New York, Rats

2004 Winners

DAVID, AMANDA. *Wonder When You'll Miss Me*. William Morrow.

After she's assaulted under the bleachers at school, the circus offers a safe haven for runaway Faith, and her Fat Girl imaginary self.

Subjects: Runaways, Rape, Revenge, Circus, Body Image

HADDON MARK. *The Curious Incident of the Dog in the Night-time*. Doubleday.

When autistic math whiz Christopher uses the investigative techniques of Sherlock Holmes to determine who killed his neighbor's dog, he also discovers family secrets.

Subjects: Autism, Savants, Mystery, England

HOSSEINI, KHALED. *The Kite Runner*. Riverhead Books.

Amir is now a successful novelist in America, but returns to Taliban-controlled Afghanistan when he feels an obligation to rescue the son of his murdered childhood friend.

Subjects: Friendship, Afghanistan, Social Class, Betrayal

NIFFENEGGER, AUDREY. *The Time Traveler's Wife*. MacAdam/Cage.

Clare is startled when her future husband drops naked into her parent's meadow, but such is the life for Clare when she falls in love with Henry, who's tossed back and forth as he travels in time.

Subjects: Time Travel, Love Story, Marriage

PACKER, Z. Z. *Drinking Coffee Elsewhere*. Riverhead Books.

The predominantly African-American characters in this debut collection of short fiction provide a fresh, ironic look at the twenty-first-century world they've inherited.

Subjects: Short Stories, African Americans

ROACH, MARY. *Stiff.* Norton. **NF**
This serious yet witty study explores the many beneficial uses of cadavers, from anatomical study to forensic medicine, crash dummies, and organ transplants.
Subjects: Human Body, Human Dissection

SALZMAN, MARK. *True Notebooks.* Knopf. **NF**
Volunteering to teach creative writing to incarcerated teens, Salzman provides them with an alternative to acting out through writing about their families, anger, and the police.
Subjects: Teaching, Creative Writing, Imprisoned Teens

SATRAPI, MARJANE. *Persepolis.* Pantheon Books. **NF**
Minimal, stark drawings reveal the author's oppressive youth in 1979 revolutionary Iran when the Shah is overthrown and an even stricter regime assumes control.
Subjects: Family, Graphic Novel, Iran, Iranian Revolution (1979)

WINSPEAR, JACQUELINE. *Maisie Dobbs.* Soho.
First in a series set in post–World War I London, Maisie Dobbs's initial private investigation reawakens memories of her wartime experiences and ill-fated romance.
Subjects: Mystery, World War I, England

YATES, BART. *Leave Myself Behind.* Kensington Books.
Moving to a small town, Noah's life becomes filled with secrets, from strange notes stuffed in Mason jars and left in the walls of his home to falling in love with a neighborhood boy.
Subjects: Gay Teens, New England

2003 Winners

BARRY, LYNDA. *One Hundred Demons.* Sasquatch Books. **NF**
Using her distinctive, stylized drawing, Barry remembers some of the demons in her life, from a cruel remark about her dancing to distinctive smells in people's homes, in a semiautobiographical work.
Subjects: Graphic Novel, Memoir

CONROY, PAT. *My Losing Season.* Doubleday/Nan A. Talese. **NF**
Best-selling author Conroy offers a play-by-play description of his senior year playing basketball for the Citadel under a coach who's almost as abusive as his father.
Subjects: Memoir, Family, Sports, Basketball, Fathers and Sons, South Carolina

FERRIS, TIMOTHY. *Seeing in the Dark: How Backyard Stargazers Are Probing Deep Space and Guarding Earth from Interplanetary Peril.* Simon & Schuster. **NF**
Ferris pays homage to the cadre of amateur astronomers who make use of

advances in telescope design and discover new objects in the sky at a rate to equal the professionals.

Subjects: Astronomy, Stars, Outer Space

FFORDE, JASPER. *The Eyre Affair*. Viking.

Before Jane Eyre meets an untimely death, literary detective Thursday Next must find and halt the serial killer who enters books and kills off literary characters.

Subjects: Fantasy, England, English Literature

LAWSON, MARY. *Crow Lake*. Dial Press.

Now a zoology professor, Kate finds it difficult to accept the sacrifices her older brothers made to raise her and her younger sister after their parents were killed in an automobile accident.

Subjects: Brothers and Sisters, Farm Life, Orphans, Family

MALLOY, BRIAN. *The Year of Ice*. St. Martin's Press.

Constantly skating on thin ice in his relationship with his irresponsible, womanizing father, high school student Kevin conceals his gay side, not realizing his father also has a secret.

Subjects: Fathers and Sons, Gay Teens

OTSUKA, JULIE. *When the Emperor Was Divine*. Alfred A. Knopf.

Returning to California after living in an internment camp during World War II, a Japanese American family reassembles their vandalized home but is unable to reconstruct their family.

Subjects: Japanese Americans, World War II, Internment Camps, California, Historical Fiction

PACKER, ANN. *The Dive from Clausen's Pier*. Alfred A. Knopf.

Her boyfriend's dive off Clausen's Pier into shallow water leaves him paralyzed and Carrie unsure what to do about their shaky relationship, until she "dives" into a potential career in New York City.

Subjects: Accidents, Wisconsin

SOUTHGATE, MARTHA. *The Fall of Rome*. Scribner.

At an exclusive prep school a solitary African-American instructor, a promising African-American student from New York City, and a divorced white English teacher form a triangle that wrestles with issues of identity, race, and integrity.

Subjects: Teachers and Students, Boarding School, African Americans

WEISBERG, JOSEPH. *10th Grade*. Random House.

A typical teen who isn't athletic, romantic, or academic, Jeremy's observations of the antics of his fellow classmates will be familiar to anyone who's ever attended high school.

Subject: High School

2002 Winners

BROOKES, GERALDINE. *Year of Wonders: A Novel of the Plague.* Viking.
After plague strikes, the townsfolk agree to stay quarantined in their village, but eventually succumb to doubt, greed, and accusations of witchery in seventeenth-century England.
Subjects: Plague, Quarantine, England, Historical Fiction

DOYLE, WILLIAM. *An American Insurrection: The Battle of Oxford, Mississippi, 1962.* Doubleday. **NF**
As the first black man to enter the University of Mississippi, James Meredith ignites battles both political and physical.
Subjects: Civil Rights, University of Mississippi, College Integration, Mississippi

DURHAM, DAVID ANTHONY. *Gabriel's Story.* Doubleday.
Unhappy about moving to a Kansas farm, Gabriel and a friend run away to join a cattle drive to Texas, but too late realize they're at the mercy of brutally immoral cowboys.
Subjects: Cowboys, African Americans, Kansas, Historical Fiction, Western

EHRENREICH, BARBARA. *Nickel and Dimed: On [Not] Getting By in Boom-time America.* Holt/Metropolitan Books. **NF**
Journalist Ehrenreich works a variety of minimum-wage jobs and presents a stark picture of living hand to mouth in this "land of opportunity."
Subjects: Working, Poverty

ENGER LEIF. *Peace Like a River.* Atlantic Monthly Press.
Sentenced to jail for killing two prowlers who threatened harm to his family, Davey Land escapes and his entire family packs up and leaves home to find him.
Subjects: Fathers and Sons, Brothers, Minnesota, Historical Fiction

KRUGER, KOBIE. *Wilderness Family: At Home with Africa's Wildlife.* Ballantine Books. **NF**
Kruger loves the wildlife around her ranger station in a remote part of South Africa, but isn't quite sure what to do with the starving lion cub her husband brings home.
Subjects: Lions, Family, South Africa

MORRISSEY, DONNA. *Kit's Law.* Houghton Mifflin.
The wild ways of her mentally challenged mother make it difficult for Kit to keep Josie out of an asylum after her protective grandmother dies.
Subjects: Mothers and Daughters, Mental Illness

ODOM, MEL. *The Rover.* Tor.
Adventures that four-foot-tall, Third Level Librarian Wick only reads about

in books become reality when he is kidnapped by pirates, sold into slavery, and forced to rob a tomb.
Subjects: Fantasy, Libraries

VIJAYARAGHAVAN, VINEETA. *Motherland.* Soho.
Raised in America, teen Maya learns about her heritage and identity when she spends a summer visiting her grandmother in India.
Subjects: Family, Grandmothers, India

WALKER, REBECCA. *Black, White, and Jewish: Autobiography of a Shifting Self.* Putnam/Riverhead Books. **NF**
Born to civil rights activists, Walker's world changes when her white Jewish father and black mother divorce, leaving her with no identity.
Subjects: Memoir, African Americans, Judaism

2001 Winners

BRADLEY, JAMES, AND RON POWERS. *Flags of Our Fathers.* Bantam. **NF**
When Bradley discovers his father is one of the six men immortalized by the famous 1945 Iwo Jima flag-raising, he sets out to learn more about the momentous event.
Subjects: Iwo Jima, Marine Corps, World War II

BRADSHAW, GILLIAN. *The Sand-reckoner.* Tor/Forge.
Figuring calculations in the sand, Archimedes combines mathematical genius and engineering expertise to design catapults for use against invading Roman soldiers during the Punic Wars.
Subjects: Archimedes, Mathematics, Engineers, Ancient Greece, Historical Fiction

CHEVALIER, TRACY. *The Girl with a Pearl Earring.* Dutton.
Could the servant Griet, who mixes pigments for Vermeer, be the unnamed girl in his famous painting "The Girl with a Pearl Earring?" If so, where did she get the earrings?
Subjects: Artists, Holland

COLTON, LARRY. *Counting Coup: A True Story of Basketball and Honor on the Little Big Horn.* Warner Books. **NF**
Life, family, and friends on the reservation distract talented basketball player Sharon LaFarge from her quest for a college scholarship.
Subjects: Sports, Basketball, Native Americans, Crow Indians, Montana

JORDAN, JUNE. *Soldier: A Poet's Childhood.* Basic Books. **NF**
Jordan's father, who vacillates between affection and sternness, makes demands that eventually transform her into a strong "little soldier."
Subjects: Memoir, African Americans, Jamaican Americans, Family, Poets

MARILLIER, JULIET. *Daughter of the Forest.* Tor.
When Sorcha's brothers are changed to swans, she must weave each a shirt from nettle plant threads to return them to human form.
Subjects: Brothers and Sisters, Quest, Self Sacrifice, Fantasy, Love Story

PHILBRICK, NATHANIEL. *In the Heart of the Sea: The Tragedy of the Whaleship Essex.* Viking. **NF**
The sinking of the Essex provides Melville the impetus for writing *Moby Dick* and later propels Philbrick into exhaustive research about the crew of the whaling ship.
Subjects: Whaling, Shipwrecks

SHERWOOD, BEN. *The Man Who Ate the 747.* Bantam Books.
Could love, rather than fame or fortune, be the reason farmer Wally Chubb is eating a 747 airplane?
Subjects: World Records, Humor, Love Story, Nebraska

STRAUSS, DARIN. *Chang and Eng: A Novel.* Dutton.
Conjoined twins Chang and Eng come to America from Thailand as freaks for a sideshow, but soon marry, farm, father children, and lead "normal" lives until death takes them both.
Subjects: Family, Brothers, Conjoined Twins

WATT, ALAN. *Diamond Dogs.* Little, Brown.
Angry Neil, a teen living with his abusive and equally angry father, must eventually talk about the classmate he hits and kills while driving drunk.
Subjects: Fathers and Sons, Drunk Driving, Secrets, Nevada

2000 Winners

BRESHEARS, DAVID. *High Exposure: An Enduring Passion for Everest and Unforgiving Places.* Simon & Schuster. **NF**
A filmmaking expedition to record an ascent to the Everest summit turns into a mass rescue as cameramen and climbers alike find themselves trapped by horrific weather.
Subjects: Mount Everest, Mountaineering, Adventure

CARD, ORSON SCOTT. *Ender's Shadow.* Tor.
Plucked from the streets, orphan Bean is sent to Battle School where his tactical combat skills pair him with the legendary Ender Wiggins and together they battle the alien buggers.
Subjects: Science Fiction, War

CLARKE, BREENA. *River, Cross My Heart.* Little, Brown.
Turned away from the white-controlled Georgetown swimming pool leads to

tragedy when the neighborhood kids swim in the treacherous Potomac River and Johnnie Mae's sister drowns.
Subjects: African Americans, Family, Washington DC, Historical Fiction

CODELL, ESME RAJI. *Educating Esme: Diary of a Teacher's First Year.* Algonquin Books. **NF**
Rookie teacher Codell upsets the school administration with her unconventional teaching, makes the lazy teachers jealous, but stimulates and excites her fifth graders to learn.
Subjects: Memoir, Teaching, Chicago

FUQUA, JONATHAN SCOTT. *The Reappearance of Sam Webber.* Bancroft Press.
When his father disappears, Sam and his mother move to a different neighborhood where he attends a new school and his only friend is the African-American janitor.
Subjects: African Americans, Friendship, Baltimore

GAIMAN, NEIL. *Stardust.* Avon/Spike.
Telling his romantic interest he'll bring her the star they watched fall leads Tristran Thorn into the land of Faerie where he discovers a new life and love.
Subjects: Fantasy, Love Story, England

GREENLAW, LINDA. *The Hungry Ocean: A Swordboat Captain's Journey.* Hyperion. **NF**
During 30 days at sea hunting swordfish, Greenlaw and her crew face uncertain weather, the danger of slippery decks, and long hours cleaning and packing away their catch.
Subjects: Fishing, Grand Banks (Newfoundland), Newfoundland

HART, ELVA TREVINO. *Barefoot Heart: Stories of a Migrant Child.* Bilingual Press/ Editorial Bilingue. **NF**
Though growing up accompanying her parents on the migrant circuit was difficult, the author eventually gives up her corporate career and returns to living in the barrio.
Subjects: Memoir, Family, Migrant Workers, Mexican Americans

HARUF, KENT. *Plainsong.* Alfred A. Knopf.
Providing a home for pregnant 17-year-old Victoria, a pair of elderly bachelor ranchers learns that the best-loved families are often composed of unrelated members.
Subjects: Family, Teen Pregnancy, Colorado

PORTER, CONNIE. *Imani All Mine.* Houghton Mifflin.
Still living in fear of her rapist, 15-year-old Tasha showers love on her daughter Imani, until a drive-by shooting squashes her dreams.
Subjects: African Americans, Teen Pregnancy, Buffalo, NY

1999 Winners

ALEXANDER, CAROLINE. *The Endurance: Shackleton's Legendary Antarctic Expedition.* Knopf. **NF**
When his wooden sailing ship becomes icebound during an attempt to cross the South Pole, Shackleton devises ways to keep his crew alive in subzero blizzards.
Subjects: Antarctica, Explorers, Adventure

BOYLAN, JENNIFER FINNEY [written as James Finney Boylan]. *Getting In.* Warner Books.
A tour of several swanky Eastern colleges quickly reveals that the adults and teens on the trip have differing ideas of what constitutes the "perfect college."
Subjects: College Admissions, Humor

DOMINICK, ANDIE. *Needles: A Memoir of Growing up with Diabetes.* Scribner. **NF**
With an older, diabetic sister, needles are as normal a part of the author's life, as are all the doctor appointments and emergency hospital visits.
Subjects: Memoir, Family, Sisters, Diabetes

GILSTRAP, JOHN. *At All Costs.* Warner.
On the run from federal agents, Jake and Carolyn are determined to prove they're innocent of murdering 16 people, especially since their teenage son is on the lam with them.
Subjects: Family, Fugitives

KERCHEVAL, JESSE LEE. *Space: A Memoir.* Algonquin. **NF**
Moving to Cocoa, Florida, in the late 1960s, Jesse notes her depressed mother's reliance on valium just as the space race, Vietnam, women's rights, and the drug culture soar into prominence.
Subjects: Memoir, Family, Outer Space, Florida

KLUGER, STEVE. *Last Days of Summer.* Avon/Bard.
In his quest to find a hero, healthy Joey Margolis writes letters to Charlie Banks, the explosive rookie third baseman playing for the 1940s NY Giants.
Subjects: Historical Fiction, Baseball, Judaism, World War II, Epistolary Novel

ROBINSON, KIM STANLEY. *Antarctica.* Bantam.
The land takes center stage as environmentalists, entrepreneurs, researchers, and tourists clash over the gradually melting realm of Antarctica.
Subjects: Antarctica, Ecology

SANTIAGO, ESMERALDA. *Almost a Woman.* Perseus/Merloyd Lawrence. **NF**
Straddling American and Puerto Rican cultures, Santiago's memoir focuses on her adolescent dreams of escaping her Brooklyn barrio.
Subjects: Memoir, Puerto Rico, Brooklyn, NY

SENNA, DANZY. *Caucasia*. Riverhead Books.

The lighter-skinned daughter of a biracial marriage, Birdie goes into hiding with her white mother where she has no choice but to give up her black heritage.
Subjects: Family, Sisters, Interracial Family, Historical Novel

SILVERBERG, ROBERT, Editor. *Legends: Short Novels by the Masters of Modern Fantasy*. Tor.

The amazing worlds created by noted authors, ranging from Anne McCaffrey's "Pern" to Steven King's "Dark Tower," are collected in these 11 novellas.
Subjects: Fantasy

1998 Winners

BODANIS, DAVID. *The Secret Family: Twenty-four Hours Inside the Mysterious Worlds of Our Minds and Bodies*. Simon & Schuster. **NF**

Thanks to scientific technology, the 24/7 operation of the inner machinery of humans is revealed, complete with photos and illustrations.
Subjects: Biology, Human Body

BRAGG RICK. *All Over but the Shoutin'*. Pantheon Books. **NF**

Bragg's climb to Pulitzer Prize distinction begins in his early years as he grows up a poor, white Southerner, living with an abusive alcoholic father and a courageous mother.
Subjects: Memoir, Family, Mothers and Sons, Alabama

CARROLL, REBBECCA, Editor. *Sugar in the Raw: Voices of Young Black Girls in America*. Crown Trade Paperbacks. **NF**

Through interviews, 15 young black women speak honestly about their personal lives, including their race, gender, and future.
Subjects: African Americans, Interviews

COOK, KARIN. *What Girls Learn*. Pantheon Books.

Quiet Tilden and her rebellious sister Elizabeth adjust first to their mother's marriage to Nick and then to her subsequent battle with breast cancer.
Subjects: Mothers and Daughters, Sisters, Breast Cancer

HAMILL, PETE. *Snow in August*. Little, Brown.

Swapping Jewish folklore for baseball stories, Rabbi Hirsch and preteen Michael Devlin enjoy a friendship that helps them defeat racial prejudice in an unusual way.
Subjects: Judaism, Friendship, Baseball, Historical Fiction, New York

JUNGER, SEBASTIAN. *The Perfect Storm: A True Story of Men Against the Sea*. Norton. **NF**

A Canadian cold front, Bermuda hurricane, and Great Lakes disturbance

converge into a killer tempest that catches the North American fishing fleet unaware of danger.
Subjects: Fishing, Storms at Sea, New England

KRAKAUER, JON. *Into Thin Air: A Personal Account of the Mt. Everest Disaster.* Villard. **NF**
   On the mountain when the 1996 climbing disaster occurs, Krakauer offers a firsthand account of the catastrophe that leads to the deaths of five climbers.
Subjects: Mount Everest, Mountaineering, Adventure

THOMAS, VELMA MAIA. *Lest We Forget: The Passage from Africa to Slavery and Emancipation.* Crown Trade Paperbacks. **NF**
   Copies of letters and newspaper clippings, enclosed in pouches and envelopes, highlight the painful experience of slavery and the hope of freedom.
Subjects: Slavery, African Americans

TRICE, DAWN TURNER. *Only Twice I've Wished for Heaven.* Crown.
   Living in a planned African-American community, friendship with fellow outsider Valerie and secret trips to Miss Jonetta's liquor store keep Tempest from boredom.
Subjects: African Americans, Community, Chicago

WILLIS, CONNIE. *To Say Nothing of the Dog; or, How We Found the Bishop's Bird Stump at Last.* Bantam Books.
   Time traveler Ned Henry is sent backward in time to restore Coventry Cathedral, destroyed in World War II, but the time travel machine keeps dispatching him to the wrong time periods.
Subjects: Time Travel, England, Humor

Chapter 4

The Edwards Award

Introductory Overview and Brief Author Introductions

Mary Arnold

Margaret Alexander Edwards was passionate about reading and adolescent readers, and this commitment inspired the first ALA/YALSA award in her honor, the Margaret A. Edwards Award. For more than 30 years, Edwards spent her professional life at the Enoch Pratt Free Library in Baltimore, Maryland, connecting teenagers and good reading, training new librarians to work with teens, and pioneering outreach services for teens as one of the original YA services advocates.

In the time before true YA literature was published, Edwards was a tireless reader in search of titles and authors that spoke to adolescent interests and needs. In her quest, she solicited suggestions and recommendations from teens themselves for books that provided both a mirror and window, books that helped young readers move beyond themselves and into a larger world. Quality writing, important themes, and compelling characters are the hallmarks of the books she recommended and discussed with readers. To understand the Edwards' philosophy for working with young adults to create lifelong readers, look no further than her inspirational book *The Fair Garden and the Swarm of Beasts: The Library and the Young Adult* (ALA Centennial Edition, 2002).

Beginning with the publication of S. E. Hinton's *The Outsiders* in 1967, a body of literature written specifically for a teen audience grew, as did the ranks of librarians who, following Margaret Edwards' example, dedicated themselves to providing excellent library services to teens. The Young Adult Services Division (YASD), established in 1957, saw the importance of establishing awards to recognize and celebrate outstanding books for teen readers. However, it was *School Library Journal* publisher Neff A. Perlman and editor in chief Lillian N.

Gerhardt who spearheaded the drive to celebrate those writers whose work, throughout time, made major contributions to young adults and their reading. Gerhardt thought that *SLJ* should sponsor such an award, and approached ALA's Young Adult Services Division (now YALSA) to develop guidelines and criteria and administer the *School Library Journal* Young Adult Author Award/ Selected and Administered by the American Library Association's Young Adult Services Division.

If you are looking to read challenged books you are in the right list!

The Edwards winners are a who's who of frequently challenged authors:

Robert Cormier	Lois Lowry	S. E. Hinton	Lois Duncan
Francesca Lia Block	Madeleine L'Engle	Chris Crutcher	Gary Paulsen
Nancy Garden	Walter Dean Myers	Paul Zindel	

And the most frequently challenged? Judy Blume

Visit the ALA Office of Intellectual Freedom's Banned Books Week Web site (www.ala .org/ala/oif/bannedbooksweek/bannedbooksweek.htm) for more information.

Starting in 1986, YALSA leaders worked with a member committee to develop guidelines and criteria for this exciting new award. Published in the *ALA Handbook of Organization* for 1991/1992 was the following initial charge: the award would be given biennially to "a living author or co-author whose book or books, over a period of time, have been accepted by young people as an authentic voice that continues to illuminate their experiences and emotions, giving insight into their lives. The book or books should enable them to understand themselves, the world in which they live, and their relationship with others and with society." The honored author would receive a citation and a $1,000 cash prize from *School Library Journal*. In 1990, YASD decided to make an award annually, and the name was changed to honor Margaret A. Edwards' reading legacy. Eventually, *SLJ* increased the amount of the cash award to $2,000, which still stands as of the printing of this book.

Which Edwards winner went on to win a Printz Award?

Walter Dean Myers

A five-member selection committee (three elected, two appointed) serves a two-year term to select a recipient for each annual award. The Margaret A. Edwards Award policies and procedures can be found on the YALSA Web site (www.ala.org/yalsa/edwards) and include the following definitions and specific criteria:

Definition of Terms

- The book or books honored must be in print at the time of nomination.
- The author(s), individual, or co-author must be living at the time of nomination and agree to accept the award during the American Library Association Annual conference in the award year.
- "Book or books" indicates titles written either specifically for a young adult reader or titles written for adults that young adults continue to request and read.
- Books eligible for citation must have been published in the United States no less than five years prior to the first meeting of the current Margaret A. Edwards Award Committee during the ALA Midwinter Meeting (for the 2006 award to Jacqueline Woodson, for example, only her books published in 2001 or earlier could be considered).
- Why five years? It's believed that period of time allows books to reach a wide level of availability and be accepted by the widest possible audience of teen readers.
- "Continues to illuminate their experiences and emotions" means the book or books have become a literary cornerstone for young adults.

Film adaptations include:

Judy Blume's *Forever* (1978)
Robert Cormier's *The Chocolate War* (1988)
Lois Duncan's *I Know What You Did Last Summer* (1997)
Madeleine L'Engle's *A Wrinkle In Time* (2003)
Legend of Earthsea (2004) based on Ursula Le Guin's *A Wizard of Earthsea and The Tombs of Atuan*

In addition to these general guidelines, the committee is charged with broad and deep reading, maintaining awareness of the entire range of books that meet the basic terms of the award. The following specific questions guide and focus the committee's work:

1. Does the book(s) help adolescents become aware of themselves and answer their questions about their role and importance in relationships, society, and in the world at large?
2. Is the book(s) of acceptable literary quality?
3. Does the book(s) satisfy the curiosity of young adults and yet help them thoughtfully build a philosophy of life?
4. Is the book(s) currently popular with a wide range of young adults in many different parts of the country?
5. Does the book(s) serve as a "window to the world" for young adults?

While these are certainly lofty and commendable guidelines, it's obvious that each committee has its work cut out for it in debating, discussing, and defining for their use exactly what "literary quality," "popularity," "philosophy of life," and "window to the world" will mean. And what exciting discussions those can be! Our 2006 committee began deliberations with an alphabetized list of potential authors for consideration, several of whom had been nominated by colleagues and teen readers. We narrowed our list by looking at each author's eligible titles, lots of reading and rereading with the criteria in mind, and spirited debate.

> Winning a lifetime achievement award doesn't mean an author stops writing. All of the Edwards winners have written more books than are listed in their award citation. Look for other titles in your library's catalog.

The excitement at Midwinter Meeting is palpable. Because award committee meetings are closed to observers, there is great anticipation for the Monday morning Youth Media Awards Press Conference, when all is revealed. When the Margaret A. Edwards committee makes a final choice, including the books that will be cited, the YALSA office provides a telephone contact for the author. Five nervous librarians huddle around the speakerphone and thrill to the honoree's first words. While it's unlikely that a committee's first choice may reluctantly turn down the award, usually because he or she cannot be available to accept the award and share a few remarks during the Edwards Award Luncheon at the annual conference, committees will have a second author name in reserve. Several authors have exclaimed over the both the honor and the idea of a "lifetime" achievement award-and are assured this does not mean that they may stop writing! In fact, authors are eligible to receive the Margaret A. Edwards award more than once, but (remember the five year rule) not more frequently than every six years. Many of the previous winners listed have continued to publish books popular with young readers, and it's interesting to speculate who will be the first "repeat" honoree.

Many of YA literature's guiding lights have been honored thus far. Each year the honoree is profiled in a cover interview in the June issue of *School Library Journal*, and the committee's wording of recognition from the citation is included on the YALSA Web site. Margaret A. Edwards seals are available from ALA Graphics to promote honored titles, and the YALSA Web site offers additional ideas to extend this award-winning reading invitation to young readers (www.ala.org/yalsa/booklists).

Edwards Award–winning Authors

Orson Scott Card (2008). An accomplished storyteller, Card weaves the everyday experiences of adolescence into broader narratives, addressing universal questions about humanity and society. *Ender's Game* (1985) presents a future where a global government trains gifted young children from around the world in the art of interstellar warfare, hoping to find a leader whose skills can prevent a second attack upon humanity by the insect-like aliens descriptively nicknamed "buggers." Young Andrew "Ender" Wiggin may be the savior they seek. As seen in the companion tale, *Ender's Shadow* (2000), Ender is not alone, as orphaned Bean relates his own Battle School experiences. Just as the stories of Ender and Bean are paralleled in the novels, their experiences echo those of teens, beginning as children navigating in an adult world and growing into a state of greater awareness of themselves, their communities, and the larger universe. *Committee Chair:* Brenna Shanks

Lois Lowry (2007). *The Giver* (1993), awarded the Newbery Medal in 1994, has been recognized as an instant classic from the time of publication. This view of a future utopia/dystopia encapsulates Lowry's major themes of the power of memory in our lives; the cycles of birth, death, and rebirth that shape our experience; and the bedrock of connection in which we share knowledge and sustenance. Jonas's ritualistic coming-of-age and discovery that the hope of security at the cost of freedom is too high a price to pay offer a provocative and complex experience for young readers. *Committee Chair:* Mary Hastler

Jacqueline Woodson (2006) has said, "I feel compelled to write against stereotypes, hoping people will see that some issues know no color, class, sexuality" (ALA, 2006). Since her seventh grade English teacher said, "You are the real thing," Woodson has used words with lyrical style to shape her response to the world, where young people must learn the source of their own power to discover hope and respond to life. Teen readers of *I Hadn't Meant to Tell You This* (1994) and its sequel *Lena* (1999), *From the Notebooks of Melanin Sun* (1995), *If You Come Softly* (1998), and *Miracle's Boys* (2000) have identified with her richly drawn characters as they struggle to grow and celebrate their unique place in the world. *Committee Chair:* Mary Arnold

Francesca Lia Block (2005). The creative daughter of artistic parents, Block's writing celebrates and immortalizes the eccentric glamour of southern California in stories of pop magical realism firmly grounded in the values of family, friendship, and commitment. *Weetzie Bat* (1989) and companions *Witch Baby* (1991), *Cherokee Bat and the Goat Guys* (1992), *Missing Angel Juan* (1993), and *Baby Be-Bop* (1996) introduced an exciting new cast of characters and settings into YA literature, "transforming gritty urban environments into a funky fairytale dream world" (ALA, 2005). *Committee Chair:* Cindy Dobrez

Ursula K. Le Guin (2004). In both the Earthsea series, *A Wizard of Earthsea* (1968), *The Tombs of Atuan* (1971), *The Farthest Shore* (1972), and *Tehanu: The*

Last Book of Earthsea (1991) and additional cited titles *The Left Hand of Darkness* (1969) and *The Beginning Place* (1980), Le Guin, fantasy writer and social activist, according to committee chair Francisca Goldsmith, "takes on issues arising from trying to live humanely in the natural world, exploring the tension between individuality and social norms." Her interest in music, dance, and water permeates the imagery of her philosophical and thought-provoking stories in which young readers continue to find meaning as they come of age. *Committee Chair:* Francisca Goldsmith

Nancy Garden (2003). *Annie on My Mind* (1982) catapulted a one-time actress and theater lighting designer into the forefront of YA literature. This sensitive and bittersweet story electrified the publishing world with its look at two young women discovering first love. Garden herself met her life partner when both were teens. *Annie* garnered awards as well as attracting controversy and censorship attempts, but Garden maintains that young readers can be trusted with new ways of thinking about our wonderfully diverse world and about one another as human beings. *Committee Chair:* Rosemary Chance

Paul Zindel (2002). By turns hilarious and strange, Zindel's books treat teens with respect for the journey toward personal identity and responsibility that adolescence demands, a journey often complicated by struggles with dysfunctional family dynamics. A science teacher and budding playwright, his *The Effect of Gamma Rays on Man-in-the-Moon Marigolds: A Drama in Two Acts* (1971) won the Pulitzer Prize. The teen characters in that work were so compelling that he was encouraged to write a novel for that audience. *The Pigman* (1968) and its sequel, *The Pigman's Legacy* (1980), as well as his personal memoir *The Pigman and Me* (1992), have earned an honored place in the lexicon of YA literature. Also cited was *My Darling, My Hamburger* (1969), which takes a cutting-edge look at teenage sexuality, personal responsibility, and the importance of positive parental influence. *Committee Chair:* Mary Long

Robert Lipsyte (2001). It was 1967 when Lipsyte was named one of only two internationally syndicated sports columnists for the *New York Times* and when he published his first novel for young adults, *The Contender*. Companion titles *The Brave* (1991) and *The Chief* (1993) continue to explore the world of boxing with a realistic, hard-hitting look at what it takes to deal with defeat and excel in sports and life. The award also recognizes *One Fat Summer* (1977), following smart—and smart-mouthed—Bobby Marks's story of personal transformation. *Committee Chair:* Jennifer Jung Gallant

Chris Crutcher (2000). Working with young people is a way of life for Crutcher, who worked until 1995 as a child and family therapist in the Pacific

Northwest. In his stories he attempts to illuminate and alleviate some of the damage and pain he's witnessed in the lives of young people, and to commend loyalty, friendship, and courage as ways to emerge from the fray of adolescence most gloriously human. The committee singled out *Running Loose* (1983), *Stotan!* (1986), *The Crazy Horse Electric Game* (1987), *Chinese Handcuffs* (1989), *Athletic Shorts* (1991), a short story collection, and *Staying Fat for Sarah Byrnes* (1993). *Committee Chair:* Joan Atkinson

Anne McCaffrey (1999). From her home in County Wicklow, Ireland, McCaffrey says, "We build the worlds we wouldn't mind living in" (Merritt, n.d.). And the science fantasy worlds of McCaffrey's imagination have invited young readers to enter and experience what it means to be human and alive. *Dragonflight* (1968), *Dragonquest* (1971), and *The White Dragon* (1978) introduce the world of Pern, with its unrelenting dangers, while the Harper Hall trilogy books, *Dragonsong* (1976), *Dragonsinger* (1977), and *Dragondrums* (1979) introduce a compelling young woman who discovers the destiny her talents demand. McCaffrey says *The Ship Who Sang* (1969) remains her personal favorite story. *Committee Chair:* Jana Fine

Madeleine L'Engle (1998), cited for the Austin Family series titles *Meet the Austins* (1960) and *A Ring of Endless Light* (1980), and the Time Fantasy series titles *A Wrinkle in Time* (1962; also won the Newbery Medal 1963) and *A Swiftly Tilting Planet* (1978), creates marvelous blends of scientific principles and fantastic elements, but the core themes remain individual courage and moral responsibility in the age-old battle between the forces of light and darkness. *Committee Chair:* Jeri C. Baker

Gary Paulsen (1997) often creates memorable characters and thrilling plots from aspects of his personal experiences, living a life built on struggle and adventure. An authentic respect and understanding of the natural world permeates *Hatchet* (1987), *The Crossing* (1987), *Canyons* (1990), *Woodsong* (1990), *The Winter Room* (1989), and *Dancing Carl* (1983), and Paulsen pits coming-of-age issues and self-discovery as part of the struggle for survival. *Committee Chair:* Helen Vandersluis

Judy Blume (1996) created a cultural milestone in realistic fiction for young adults with *Forever* (1975). Its frank and compassionate look at first love and awakening sexuality has, over the years, touched many, many young readers, and has touched off successive rounds of censorship challenges. Blume recognized that young people deserve the truth, that as adolescents begin to explore their own sexuality they also need to understand the responsibility for choices and the feelings of others that come with that new part of being human. *Committee Chair:* Marilee Foglesong

Cynthia Voigt (1995) touched a chord in young readers who embraced the characters in the Tillerman cycle of books. Cited are *Homecoming* (1981), *Dicey's Song* (1982), *A Solitary Blue* (1983), and *The Runner* (1985), with related themes of welcoming new experiences and learning what past events and memories are of value and what must be discarded in order to move on. The committee also cited *Building Blocks* (1984) and *Izzy Willy Nilly* (1986), which explore how family relationships and unexpected challenges affect young lives, and *Jackaroo* (1985), historical fiction in which a strong, determined young woman discovers a way to make choices that shape her future. *Committee Chair:* Joann G. Mondowney

Walter Dean Myers (1994) grew up in Harlem when it was a cultural hub for African Americans. After dropping out of school and a stint in the army, Myers, following the lead of James Baldwin, Langston Hughes, and others, began shaping his own life experiences into books whose memorable characters became fast friends to a generation of young readers. *Hoops* (1981), *Motown and Didi* (1984), *Fallen Angels* (1988), and *Scorpions* (1988) introduce young people who discover the important role supportive friends and family play as they navigate the often dark realities and temptations of urban life. Six years later, Myers would win the inaugural Michael L. Printz Award for *Monster*, making him the only author thus far to win both the Printz and the Edwards Awards. *Committee Chair:* Judy T. Nelson

M. E. Kerr (Marijane Meaker) (1993) doesn't recall a time when she didn't want to write, and filtering experience through a storyteller's eye gave her novels for teens the authentic emotional resonance that connects with successive generations of readers. *Dinky Hocker Shoots Smack* (1972), *Gentlehands* (1978), *Night Kites* (1986), and the autobiographical short story collection *Me Me Me Me Me: Not a Novel* (1983) all offer readers windows into other lives, other social worlds, and explore with sensitivity the sometimes painful, sometimes funny reality for teen outsiders. *Committee Chair:* Marion H. Hargrove

Lois Duncan (1992) is not only an author perennially popular with teen readers, but a writer who recognizes the pivotal role of peer pressure in young lives and whose characters and themes reiterate that our actions matter, and individual responsibility matters. Tense thrillers *I Know What You Did Last Summer* (1973), *Killing Mr. Griffin* (1978), *Ransom* (1966), *Summer of Fear* (1976), and *The Twisted Window* (1987), as well as her autobiographical *Chapters, My Growth As a Writer* (1982), show Duncan's connections with her reading audience through a grasp of adolescent culture. Eerie correlations between the murder of her daughter, Kait, and her own books have, sadly, kept Duncan from writing further YA suspense. *Committee Chair:* Betty Carter

Robert Cormier (1991) began writing fiction while working as a journalist in small-town Massachusetts, the setting for many of his award-winning novels. The Edwards committee cited *The Chocolate War* (1974), *I Am the Cheese* (1977), and *After the First Death* (1979), titles that exemplify Cormier's uncompromising, complex, and challenging look at the hard truths adolescents must face and the ethical and moral decisions they must make. *Committee Chair:* Ellen Ramsay

Richard Peck (1990) was the second Edwards honoree (when the award was given biennially). A stint in the military, a career as a high school classroom teacher, and warm memories of his early Illinois years paved the way for Peck's emergence as a writer for teens in his "third" career. The Edwards committee cited *Are You in the House Alone?* (1976), *Father Figure* (1978), *The Ghost Belonged to Me* (1975), *Ghosts I Have Been* (1977), *Remembering the Good Times* (1985), and *Secrets of the Shopping Mall* (1979), books exhibiting a wide range of genres and appeal, from realistic teenage problem novels and supernatural thrillers to witty satires of teen angst. All respect and celebrate the importance of relationships to young adults, and the necessity, sometimes painful, to achieve individual autonomy. *Committee Chair:* Roger Sutton

(No award given in 1989)

S. E. (Susan Eloise) Hinton (1988) is often called the grande dame of YA literature. A Midwestern teenager herself when her groundbreaking novel about the real lives of the teens she knew, *The Outsiders*, was published in 1967, Hinton's award also cited *That Was Then, This Is Now* (1971), *Rumble Fish* (1975), *Tex* (1979), and *Taming the Star Runner* (1988). Hinton wrote the kind of books about the kind of people she couldn't find on library shelves, and she paved the way for a new kind of hard-hitting, truthful YA literature. The 1988 committee lauded Hinton's books for their realism, allowing readers to explore the adolescent longing for independence while acknowledging the importance of loyalty, connection, and caring. *Committee Chair:* Susan Tait

References

American Library Association. 1991. *ALA Handbook of Organization, 1991–92.* Chicago: ALA.

American Library Association. 2004. "2005 Margaret A. Edwards Award Winner" [press release]. Available: http://www.ala.org/ala/yalsa/booklistsawards/ margaretaedwards/maeprevious/04ursula.cfm.

American Library Association. 2005. "2005 Margaret A. Edwards Award Winner" [press release]. Available: http://www.ala.org/ala/yalsa/booklistsawards/ margaretaedwards/maeprevious/05block.cfm.

American Library Association. 2006. "Jacqueline Woodson is the recipient of the 2006 Margaret A. Edwards Award" [press release]. Available: http://www.ala.org/ala/yalsa/booklistsawards/margaretaedwards/maeprevious/06.cfm.

Edwards, Margaret A. 2002. *The Fair Garden and the Swarm of Beasts: The Library and the Young Adult*, Centennial edition. Chicago: ALA Editions.

Merritt, Byron. n.d. "An Interview with Anne McCaffrey, the Creator of the *Dragonriders of Pern Series*." FWOMP (Fiction Writers of the Monterey Peninsula) Interview. Available: http://www.fwomp.com/int_ann_mccaf.htm.

YALSA. "Margaret A. Edwards Award." Available: www.ala.org/yalsa/edwards.

YALSA. "YALSA Booklists and Book Awards." Available: www.ala.org/yalsa/booklists.

The Edwards Winners: An Annotated Bibliography

Pam Spencer Holley

2008 Winner: Orson Scott Card

Ender's Game. Tor Books, 1985.
Humanity's fate rests on young Ender Wiggins, a student at Battle School, where the smartest children on Earth are trained to fight the alien insects intent on colonizing the planet.
Subjects: Brothers and Sisters, Genetic Engineering, War Games

Ender's Shadow. Tor Books, 2000.
Plucked from the streets, orphan Bean is sent to Battle School where his tactical combat skills pair him with the legendary Ender Wiggins and together they battle the alien buggers.
Subjects: Science Fiction, War

2007 Winner: Lois Lowry

The Giver. Houghton Mifflin, 1993.
As Jonas receives the memories of his community from "the Giver," he realizes his family and friends are unable to value life because they've never experienced it.
Subject: Science Fiction

2006 Winner: Jacqueline Woodson

Miracle's Boys. Putnam, 2000.
Milagro dies and her three sons react differently—the youngest weeps easily, the oldest resents giving up college, and the middle son acts as though he wants to return to juvie.
Subjects: Family, Brothers

Lena. Delacorte Press, 1999.

Lena endures her father's abuse, but when she sees the same pattern developing with her younger sister she knows running away can't be any worse than life at home.

Subjects: Runaway Teens, Sisters

If You Come Softly. Putnam, 1998.

Being in love for the first time is special, unless you're black Jeremiah and white Ellie and must contend with racism and police brutality.

Subjects: African Americans, Family, New York, Interracial Dating

From the Notebooks of Melanin Sun. Blue Sky Press, 1995.

African-American Melanin can't believe that his mother plans to disrupt their cozy twosome of a family just because she loves some white woman named Kristen.

Subjects: African Americans, Lesbian Relationship, Mothers and Sons

I Hadn't Meant to Tell You This. Delacorte, 1994.

A warm but unusual friendship develops between popular black Marie and white newcomer Lena, who are linked by the loss of their mothers and Lena's horrific secret.

Subjects: African Americans, Fathers and Daughters, Friendship, Incest, Sexual Abuse

2005 Winner: Francesca Lia Block

Baby Be-Bop. HarperCollins, 1995.

In Dirk's pre-Weetzie days he is badly beaten by gay bashers and slumps into unconsciousness; dreaming of stories told by his loving ancestors helps him heal.

Subjects: Gay Teens, Los Angeles, Ghosts, Magic Realism, Punks, Gay Bashing

Missing Angel Juan. HarperCollins, 1993.

Witch Baby follows Juan to New York City where she meets Weetzie's father's ghost who helps her find Angel Juan—just when he wants to be found.

Subjects: Ghosts, New York, Magic Realism, Drug Addiction

Cherokee Bat and the Goat Guys. HarperCollins, 1992.

Cherokee raises Witch Baby's spirits by starting up a band, but magical costumes and instruments can't guarantee success.

Subjects: Rock Music, Bands, Drugs, Magic Realism

Witch Baby. HarperCollins, 1991.

Left on Weetzie Bat's doorstep, Witch Baby becomes part of the family, but not knowing her parents makes her question who she is and why she acts like a "witch baby."

Subjects: Los Angeles, Family, Magic Realism

Weetzie Bat. Harper & Row, 1989.
>   Frustrated that neither she nor her best friend Dirk find their true loves, Weetzie makes a wish and discovers her Secret Agent Lover Man while Dirk meets Duck.

Subjects: Friendship, Los Angeles, Magic Realism

2004 Winner: Ursula K. Le Guin

Tehanu: The Last Book of Earthsea. Atheneum, 1990.
>   Adopted and trained by Tenar, Therru earns her name Tehanu when she is able to call the dragon Kalessin, which saves Tenar and Ged from an evil wizard.

Subjects: Fantasy, Magic, Dragons

The Beginning Place. Harper & Row, 1980.
>   Hugh and Irena find that idyllic Tembreabrezi is a peaceful refuge, so when their retreat is threatened, these two outsiders are primed to help.

Subjects: Science Fiction, Love

The Farthest Shore, Earthsea Trilogy, Book 3. Atheneum, 1972.
>   Ged helps Arren discover why wizards have lost their spell-casting powers on a journey that restores equilibrium to the world but leaves Ged powerless.

Subjects: Fantasy, Wizards, Magic

The Tombs of Atuan, Earthsea Trilogy, Book 2. Atheneum, 1971.
>   Serving the evil Nameless Ones, Tenar/Arha is taken from the dark underground by Ged/Sparrowhawk and realizes the combination of dark with light makes her whole.

Subjects: Fantasy, Quest, Treasure, Wizards, Priestess

The Left Hand of Darkness. Walker, 1969.
>   Sent as an envoy to Karhide, Genly Ai has difficulty dealing with its androgynous inhabitants who can assume either male or female characteristics.

Subjects: Science Fiction, Gender, Androgyny, Alien Worlds

A Wizard of Earthsea, Earthsea Trilogy, Book 1. Parnassus Press, 1968.
>   Trained as a powerful magician, Ged/Sparrowhawk calls up a spirit from the dead whose attack leaves him hovering between life and death.

Subjects: Fantasy, Wizards, Journey

2003 Winner: Nancy Garden

Annie on My Mind. Farrar, Straus, Giroux, 1982.
>   First meeting at the Metropolitan Museum of Art, Liza and Annie live in different social and economic worlds, but each slowly accepts her love for the other.

Subjects: High School, Lesbian Relationship

2002 Winner: Paul Zindel

The Pigman & Me. HarperCollins, 1992.
Zindel tells of meeting his own "Pigman" during his teen years—a friend's father who listens to his troubles, teaches him to fight, and then cooks him tasty Italian dinners.
Subjects: Authors, Memoir

The Pigman's Legacy. Harper & Row, 1980.
Still feeling guilty about Mr. Pignati's death, John and Lorraine befriend an old man they find squatting in the Pigman's former house.
Subjects: Friendship, Senior Citizen, High School

The Effect of Gamma Rays on Man-in-the-Moon Marigolds: A Drama in Two Acts. Harper & Row, 1971.
Tillie's science fair project illustrates the deadly effect of too large a dose of gamma rays compared to a moderate amount which produces large, showy, man-in-the-moon marigolds. Pulitzer Prize winner loosely based on Zindel's life.
Subjects: Family, Sisters, Mothers and Daughters, Abusive Parents

My Darling, My Hamburger. Harper & Row, 1969.
Their teacher advises them to suggest getting a hamburger when make-out sessions becomes too steamy, but Liz and Maggie find her advice doesn't always work.
Subjects: Teen Couples, High School

The Pigman. Harper & Row, 1968.
House-sitting for Mr. Pignati while he's hospitalized, teens John and Lorraine throw a party that grows out of control and leads to Mr. Pignati's fatal heart attack.
Subjects: Friendship, Betrayal, Senior Citizen, High School, New York

2001 Winner: Robert Lipsyte

The Chief. HarperCollins, 1993.
Now a police sergeant, Alfred Brooks sends aspiring Native American boxer Sonny Bear to Donatelli's gym, which begins Bear's upward climb in boxing circles.
Subjects: Native Americans, Boxing

The Brave. HarperCollins, 1991.
Cheated of his amateur crown, Sonny Bear is ready to give up boxing, but realizes his prowess in the ring can help his family and friends who live on the reservation.
Subjects: Native Americans, Boxing

One Fat Summer. Harper & Row, 1977.
Resigned to teasing about his obesity, Bobby spends his summer mowing Dr. Kahn's never-ending lawn and dreams of candy, cookies, and cake with every step.
Subjects: Obesity, Body Image

The Contender. Harper & Row, 1967.

High school dropout Alfred takes boxing lessons from Mr. Donatelli where he learns that showing up and being a contender is more important than winning.

Subjects: Boxing, African Americans, Harlem

2000 Winner: Chris Crutcher

Staying Fat for Sarah Byrnes. Greenwillow Books, 1993.

Swimming to slim down as well as to accompany his badly scarred friend Sarah, Eric sticks by her even when he's slender and she stops talking.

Subjects: Swimming, Friendship, Mental Illness

Athletic Shorts. Greenwillow Books, 1991.

If you haven't met Telephone Man or fat Angus Bethune from Crutcher's novels, this collection of short stories provides the perfect introduction.

Subjects: Sports, Short Stories

Chinese Handcuffs. Greenwillow Books, 1989.

Together triathlon star Dillon and basketball star Jennifer overcome the trauma of sibling suicide, abandonment, and incest.

Subjects: Suicide, Sexual Abuse, Athletes, Friendship

The Crazy Horse Electric Game. Greenwillow Books, 1987.

Running away from his Montana home after an injury robs him of athletic talent, Willie regains his mental and physical ability but wonders if he can return to his family.

Subjects: Runaways, Disability, African Americans

Stotan! Greenwillow Books, 1986.

Four teens discover their inner strength as they face challenges greater than they, or their swim coach, ever expected during Stotan Week.

Subjects: Swimming, High School

Running Loose. Greenwillow Books, 1983.

Louie faces the scorn of his classmates when he refuses to play for an immoral coach, unaware that bleaker days lie ahead.

Subjects: Football, Sportsmanship, Idaho

1999 Winner: Anne McCaffrey

Dragondrums, Harper Hall Trilogy, Book 3. Atheneum, 1979.

Upset when his beautiful singing voice changes, Piemur runs away to the Southern Continent, accompanied by a stolen fire lizard and his runnerbeast.

Subjects: Fantasy, Dragons, Music, Adventure

The White Dragon, Dragonriders of Pern, Book 3. Ballantine Books, 1978.
   Though the white dragon Ruth shouldn't even exist, and Jaxom shouldn't
   have impressed her, he and Ruth soon become an experienced dragon-rider
   team.
Subjects: Fantasy, Dragons, Adventure

Dragonsinger, Harper Hall Trilogy, Book 2. Atheneum, 1977.
   As the Master Harper's special apprentice, Menolly discovers she has to learn
   about music and how to get along with harpers who are jealous of her talent.
Subjects: Fantasy, Dragons, Music, Adventure

Dragonsong, Harper Hall Trilogy, Book 1. Atheneum, 1976.
   Menolly runs away after an injury prevents her from playing musical instruments, but then meets and eventually awes Pern's Master Harper with her
   melodic compositions.
Subjects: Fantasy, Dragons, Music, Adventure

Dragonquest. Dragonriders of Pern, Book 2. Ballantine Books, 1971.
   As the periods of threadfall increase, dragonrider F'lar searches for ways to
   better protect Pern and its citizens.
Subject: Fantasy

The Ship Who Sang. Walker, 1969.
   Born physically but not mentally disabled, Helva is technologically enhanced
   to become a scout ship that spends centuries searching for the perfect partner
   to fly her.
Subject: Science Fiction

Dragonflight, Dragonriders of Pern, Book 1. Walker, 1969, c1968.
   Her family killed and her position now that of a servant, Lessa's opportunities change when she meets dragonrider F'lar who searches for potential
   dragonriders.
Subject: Fantasy

1998 Winner: Madeleine L'Engle

A Ring of Endless Light. Farrar Straus Giroux, 1980.
   Vicky struggles with the deaths of friends and relatives, until one boyfriend
   steps forward and helps break the spell of darkness surrounding her.
Subjects: Dolphins, Death

A Swiftly Tilting Planet. Farrar Straus Giroux, 1978.
   Halting the threat of nuclear war falls to Charles Wallace Murry, whose time
   travels eventually alter the personality of a militaristic South American dictator.
Subjects: Fantasy, Time Travel

A Wrinkle in Time. Farrar Straus Giroux, 1962.
	After a visit by celestial time travelers, siblings Meg and Charles Wallace Murry prove the power of love when they travel along "a wrinkle in time" to rescue their father.
Subjects: Family, Fantasy, Space Travel

Meet the Austins. Vanguard Press, 1960.
	Family life at the Austins turns upside down when their orphaned cousin, manipulative Maggie, moves into their lives and their home.
Subjects: Family, Orphans

1997 Winner: Gary Paulsen

Canyons. Delacorte Press, 1990.
	Brennan Cole discovers the skull of Coyote Runs, a young Apache brave shot on his first raid, whose agitated spirit is eventually laid to rest in a favorite canyon.
Subjects: Native Americans, Apache Indians, Texas

Woodsong. Bradbury Press, 1990. **NF**
	Author Paulsen and his sled dogs train in the frozen Minnesota winter for their first attempt at running the Iditarod Sled Race in Alaska's wilderness.
Subjects: Dogsledding, Sled Dogs, Dogs, Minnesota

Winter Room. Orchard Books, 1989.
	Sitting in the fire-lit winter room, two brothers forget about the snow and ice and listen with delight to the stories Uncle David shares of a legendary lumberjack.
Subjects: Farm Life, Norwegian Americans, Logging, Minnesota

The Crossing. Orchard Books, 1987.
	An emotionally disturbed American soldier and a young Mexican boy, both of whom hope for a better life, cross paths and ironically attain their dreams.
Subjects: Mexico, Illegal Immigration, Vietnam War Veteran

Hatchet. Bradbury Press, 1987.
	After his pilot suffers a fatal heart attack and the plane crashes into a Canadian lake, sole survivor Brian Robeson swims ashore with only a windbreaker and a hatchet.
Subjects: Survival, Wilderness, Canada

Dancing Carl. Bradbury Press, 1983.
	One winter Carl works at the town's skating rink, dancing around the ice in a way that mesmerizes Willy and Marsh, two young boys who discover Carl's secret.
Subjects: Ice-skating, Minnesota

1996 Winner: Judy Blume

Forever. Bradbury Press, 1975.

Teenager Katherine thinks she'll love Michael forever, but after a summer apart, forever doesn't seem as everlasting.

Subjects: Love Story, First Love, Dating, Relationships, Sexuality

1995 Winner: Cynthia Voigt

Jackaroo, Kingdom Cycle, Book 1. Atheneum, 1985.

Donning the disguise of Jackaroo, a legendary "Robin Hood" character, Gwyn plans to help the poor but discovers she is not the only one masquerading with that intent.

Subjects: Historical Fiction, Mystery, Adventure

The Runner, Tillerman Family Cycle. Atheneum, 1985.

The Vietnam War rages, his family's farm requires his help, and his father makes impossible demands. "Bullet's" salvation is his running.

Subjects: Sports, Running, Family, Friendship

Building Blocks. Atheneum, 1984.

Frustrated that his father never stands up to his mother, Brann sees another side when he travels back in time and observes his father as a ten-year-old.

Subjects: Fathers and Sons, Time Travel

A Solitary Blue. Atheneum, 1983.

Abandoned by his mother when he is only seven, Jeff is raised by his unemotional father but finally realizes that love doesn't need to be showy or demonstrative.

Subjects: Fathers and Sons, Divorce

Dicey's Song, Tillerman Family Cycle. Atheneum, 1982.

In this sequel to *Homecoming,* it's hard for Dicey to relinquish her parental role to her eccentric grandmother Abigail, though she savors the idea of time on her own.

Subjects: Brothers and Sisters, Family

Homecoming, Tillerman Family Cycle. Atheneum, 1981.

Abandoned by their mother, Dicey shepherds her three younger siblings on a journey until they find a home with a grandmother they never knew they had.

Subjects: Family, Survival, Brothers and Sisters

1994 Winner: Walter Dean Myers

Fallen Angels. Scholastic, 1988.

Seventeen-year-old Richie Perry quickly discovers that even the streets of Harlem didn't prepare him for the grim reality of the body bags, bugs, and napalm of the Vietnam War.

Subjects: Vietnam War, African Americans

Scorpions. Harper & Row, 1988.
With his older brother in jail, Jamal reluctantly assumes leadership of the Scorpions gang, a far cry from his dream of becoming an artist.
Subjects: Gangs, African Americans, New York

Motown and Didi. Viking Kestrel, 1984.
Didi wants to escape from Harlem and attend college while Motown works hard at low-paying jobs to remain independent. Together they keep their dreams alive.
Subjects: Drug Abuse, African Americans, New York

Hoops. Delacorte Press, 1981.
Hoping that basketball will be his ticket to college and the NBA, Lonnie worries that Coach Cal will revert to his gambling habits and blow the team's final championship game.
Subject: Basketball

1993 Winner: M. E. Kerr

Night Kites. Harper & Row, 1986.
When Erick learns that his older brother Pete has returned home to die of AIDS, he's glad for the understanding of his nonconformist girlfriend Nicki.
Subjects: Brothers, AIDS (Disease)

Me Me Me Me Me: Not a Novel. Harper & Row, 1983. **NF**
An autobiographical account of the author's life in which Kerr shares some of the life stories that inspire and contribute to her writing.
Subjects: Authors, Memoir

Gentlehands. Harper & Row, 1978.
What are you supposed to do when you discover that your beloved, cultured grandfather is a Nazi war criminal?
Subjects: Grandfathers, War Criminals, Nazis

Dinky Hocker Shoots Smack! Harper & Row, 1972.
Dinky's do-gooder mother neglects her until their city's sidewalks and buildings are emblazoned with "DINKY HOCKER SHOOTS SMACK."
Subjects: Body Image, Friendship, Family

1992 Winner: Lois Duncan

The Twisted Window. Delacorte, 1987.
Tracy agrees to help Brad retrieve his little sister Mindy from their stepfather, but too late realizes that Brad is crazy and there's a search warrant for their arrest.
Subjects: Kidnapping, Mystery, Suspense

Chapters: My Growth as a Writer. Little, Brown, 1982. **NF**
   Beginning with the first story she wrote in kindergarten, author Duncan
   shares those tales that chronicle her beginning stages as a writer.
Subjects: Authors, Memoir

Killing Mr. Griffin. Little Brown, 1978.
   Convinced their English teacher is unfair, five students decide to kidnap and
   frighten him, not realizing that Mr. Griffin has a heart condition.
Subjects: Teachers and Students, Murder

Summer of Fear. Little, Brown, 1976.
   Orphaned Julia comes to live with Rachel's family and immediately charms
   everyone, except for Rachel and her dog Trickle, who have good reason to dis-
   trust her.
Subjects: Witches

I Know What You Did Last Summer. Little, Brown, 1973.
   Four friends make a pact to never tell of the horrible incident that occurred
   last summer, but someone else knows and threatens to reveal their secret.
Subjects: Mystery, Secrets, Suspense

Ransom. Doubleday, 1966.
   Being kidnapped while on your school bus is frightening, but even worse for
   five students is wondering if their parents will even pay the ransom
   demanded.
Subjects: Kidnapping, Mystery

1991 Winner: Robert Cormier

After the First Death. Pantheon Books, 1979.
   Determined to prove he's worthy of being called a terrorist, 16-year-old Miro
   helps capture a busload of small children, but feels qualms about the necessity of killing.
Subjects: Terrorism, Fathers and Sons

I Am the Cheese. Knopf, 1977.
   Adam Farmer and his family are part of a witness protection program that
   seems to do more harm than good in a work where fantasy and reality
   coexist.
Subjects: Mystery

The Chocolate War. Pantheon Books, 1974.
   When Jerry refuses to sell chocolates for a school fund-raiser, he unleashes
   the wrath of some of the Catholic faculty and a group of student bullies.
Subjects: High School, Bullies, Conformity

1990 Winner: Richard Peck

Remembering the Good Times. Delacorte Press, 1985.
Buck, Kate, and Trav are an unlikely but close-knit trio, so when Trav commits suicide, Buck and Kate are left behind to "remember the good times."
Subjects: Friendship, Suicide

Secrets of the Shopping Mall. Delacorte Press, 1979.
Escaping from a gang, Bernie and Theresa wind up living in the department store of a suburban mall, but may not be the only sentient bodies residing there.
Subjects: Gangs, Shopping Malls

Father Figure. Viking Press, 1978.
When Jim and his younger brother Byron reunite with their estranged father, the biggest problem is deciding who will be the "father figure" for Byron.
Subjects: Fathers and Sons, Brothers

Ghosts I Have Been. Viking Press, 1977.
Snubbed by the rich girls in her class, Blossom Culp makes friends with ghosts and her wealthy classmate Alexander Armsworth, who also has the gift of second sight.
Subjects: Ghosts, Supernatural

Are You in the House Alone? Viking Press, 1976.
When a rich, popular student harasses and then rapes Gail Osborne, no one believes her.
Subjects: Rape, Stalkers

The Ghost Belonged to Me. Viking Press, 1975.
Alexander Armsworth doubts there's a ghost living in his barn until she tells him how to prevent a train wreck.
Subjects: Ghosts, Supernatural

(No Award Given in 1989)

1988 Winner: S. E. Hinton

Tex. Delacorte Press, 1979.
Life's not easy for Tex and his brother Mason with their father away at rodeos: selling their horses is only the first step Mason takes for the brothers to survive.
Subject: Brothers

Rumble Fish. Delacorte Press, 1975.
When his older, delinquent brother Motorcycle Boy flees criminal charges, Rusty-James is left on his own with neither the skills nor the smarts needed to survive.
Subjects: Brothers, Gangs

That Was Then, This Is Now. Viking, 1971.
>
Twelve-year-old Byron adores his foster brother Mark, which makes it so hard to turn him in for selling drugs.
>
Subject: Friendship

The Outsiders. Viking, 1967.
>
Conflict between two gangs, the privileged Socs and the poor Greasers, leads to the death of Ponyboy's best friend and the beginning of a new age in teen literature.
>
Subjects: Brothers, Gangs, Friendship

The Edwards Awards Acceptance Speeches

Lois Lowry, 2007 Margaret A. Edwards Award

Lois Lowry, the 2007 Margaret A. Edwards recipient, muses on the mythic qualities and the popular longevity of her 1993 novel The Giver *and ponders the phenomenon of an author's work taking on a life of its own.*

A PASSIONATE YEARNING

I started writing this speech on a recent Wednesday, and as I sat there staring mindlessly at the computer . . . trying to think about what to say (what NEW to say!) . . . I decided to look on Amazon for the current ranking of *The Giver.*

Writers do this. It's like touching your child's forehead to feel its temperature, sniffing the bottle of milk to determine whether it is fresh, glancing up at the clouds before deciding to take an umbrella. Just a quick assessment of status.

The Giver, on Amazon, on this particular Wednesday, was ranked #573.

You may not be aware of how astounding that is. #573 on Amazon is practically a bestseller. And yet this book was published FOURTEEN years ago. To put things into perspective, I checked the ranking of *The Higher Power of Lucky,* this year's Newbery winner. It was #1,078. (Of course, it has that controversial scrotum in it.) I checked an all-time favorite, *Holes,* another Newbery book, a well-regarded film. It was #20,373. I checked *Bridge to Terabithia.* Newbery. Currently a very popular movie. #23,366. And finally, knowing for certain that I could find something that would put *The Giver* into perspective, bring it down a peg, humble it, I looked up *To Kill a Mockingbird.* It was #2,220.

Astounding.

I began to try to think about why *The Giver* has remained so popular, so meaningful to so many people, for so many years . . . why this organization has chosen to honor it, and me. And I do have some thoughts about that. But first I want to talk about what a pleasure it is to be here in the company of librarians. One of my happiest childhood memories is of going frequently to the public library in the small college town where I lived. It seemed the grandest building in the town, though there were other impressive ones nearby: the buildings of the college itself, and the law school. The bank where my grandfather's office was. But it was the library, the J. Herman Bosler Memorial Library, that had captured my heart and in which I spent so many solitary and supremely happy hours.

At home, while my sister played "school" with her dolls, frowning at them and scolding them as she taught them to read and add and multiply and sit still, I played a game that I thought of simply as "library." I arranged my books (and I was lucky to grow up in a home that valued books, and bought books, and gave me books) carefully. I stacked them up, sorted them, checked them out to my dolls and stuffed animals with great solemnity and with those magical thumps that seemed important in that pre-computer era. Thump. Thump. And the book became the property of that doll, or bear, or elephant, and I would send it off to a corner of the room with the book propped against its stuffed lap or knees.

I outgrew the dolls, of course, but never outgrew the books, or the library, though I said good-bye to that town, and that library, when I was eleven years old, in 1948, and moved on to others and to others and to others. But I remembered the J. Herman Bosler Memorial Library as being a magnificent building, something on the order of a cathedral, with pillars, and at least a hundred granite steps.

But a few years ago they invited me back to speak at the one hundredth birthday party for that library. It surprised me that the library was actually small. The steps were cement, and there were no more than ten of them. Just now I Googled it, and found this description:

> As a lasting memorial to Mr. Bosler, his widow and five children erected a handsome public library building . . . known as "The J. Herman Bosler Memorial Library." Entirely completed and equipped with furniture and books, it was formally transferred to trustees on Jan. 30, 1900, together with an endowment fund of $20,000. . . . The building has a frontage on West High Street of 57 feet and a depth of 88 feet, standing on a lot 63 by 110 feet. About 4,400 books are now upon its shelves under the care of the efficient and popular librarian, W. Homer Ames.

It is the trick that memory plays, isn't it? The enormity that we remember comes more from our emotional attachment to things than to actual size. Grandpa's lap—the place I curled so often, as he read Kipling to me—is remembered as soft and comfortable. Could it be that he might have had, actually, bony knees and scratchy tweed trousers? Could my beloved library, the cathedral of my earliest literate life, have actually had a frontage of just fifty-seven feet?

I also, incidentally, found this, as part of the library's history: "The price of a library subscription in 1900 cost $1.00 per year. The rules stated that 'all persons above the age of twelve years, of cleanly habits and good reputation may use the books in the building.'" That age rule must have changed because I was well under twelve (of cleanly habits, usually, though, and I think my reputation was good) when I prowled the stacks of that library so contentedly in the 1940s. It's probably not surprising that when I sat down to write the book that would be called *The Giver*, and to create a world that had lost so much of importance . . . it was a world that had no books.

My own first book was published when I was forty. My thirty-fourth book has just been published and I'm seventy now. I've turned them out in somewhat the same way I turned out babies, in 1958, 1959, 1961, and 1962: close together, one after another, and proud of each one of them . . . but the best part is to watch them go out into the world, and to see what they become to others.

Last weekend I sat in a large audience and watched a daughter receive a masters degree. I felt proud of her, how hard she had worked, how well she had done. But I never once felt: *I made her what she is today*. And I don't feel that way, either, about books I've written. I turn them loose. They're on their own. They take on a life separate from me. And it's the life of one book that I'm here to talk about.

Not long ago I got an e-mail from a teacher in South Carolina who told me that she teaches in a rural part of the state, a dirt-poor area. During the winter she was reading *The Giver* aloud to the class, one chapter a day. One day it snowed. A rare occurrence in South Carolina, and schools closed. During the day, when she was at home, her phone rang. She said it was the most troubled, most troublesome, most disruptive boy in her eighth grade class. We've all known those boys: sullen, disaffected, unresponsive. Yet here he was, on the phone. And he begged her to read the next chapter of *The Giver* to him. The teacher told me that she almost wept as she read to him that snowy afternoon, sitting alone in her house and hearing the boy's breath through the phone as he listened. It was the first time the boy had ever become engaged, interested, enthusiastic about *anything*.

And so I am back to the earlier question . . . what is it, about this particular book?

What was it to the young Trappist monk who wrote to me once, and told me that in the silence and solitude of his order, he had read *The Giver* and considered it a sacred text? Or the privileged high school senior who risked punishment because he insisted on reading the entire book aloud, nonstop, standing on the auditorium stage of his Minneapolis private school, refusing to obey the teachers who ordered him to stop and to return to class? How about the young woman who—not sure of how copyright law applied—asked my permission to have a page of *The Giver* tattooed on her left shoulder? And what made it appeal to a troubled adolescent in the rural south?

Well, just last week I got an e-mail from a college student, a girl who was writing a term paper using *The Giver* as what she called "contemporary myth." She asked me if I agreed with that assessment. I confessed to her that I didn't know, that I hadn't a clue what she meant by "contemporary myth" but that I was sure her paper would be intriguing and I wished her well. Then, thinking about it after I had replied to her, I tilted back my chair so that I could reach my bookcase and I pulled out Joseph Campbell, began to skim, and realized it indeed answered the question of *what is it about this particular book?*

I certainly didn't think in grandiose terms—no thoughts at all about religion or politics or philosophy—when I sat down simply intending to write a story, the story that became *The Giver*. I had been thinking a great deal about memory because I had been watching my father's diminish and fade at the same time that I watched my mother cling tenaciously, fiercely to the tiniest memories that went back seventy and eighty years and meant so much to her. So I thought about what memory means, what it does, how we use it—and of course, what would happen if we let go of it. If we *chose* to do that. I sat down to write a story that grappled with those questions. I chose to make the story about a boy. And without planning or intending it, I re-created the classic hero of all recurrent myth: the figure (and yes, though it is sexist, the mythic hero seems always to be male) who perceives something wrong in the world and who therefore is compelled to undertake a quest.

Picture the boy in South Carolina. I know nothing about him beyond what his teacher told me. He's an eighth grader. He's disruptive, disaffected, disadvantaged. He'll be a dropout soon. But I am a very visual person. My mind creates images. I picture him African American. I don't know his ethnicity, but I know where he lives—a place with a largely African-American population—and that's how he appears in my mind. I see a lanky black boy with large sneakers, restless legs, bored eyes, forced to sit in a classroom with inadequate resources—this is a poor rural area—a classroom with nothing that seems relevant to him, nothing that holds his interest. I see him sprawled at his desk, legs in the aisle. I see him yawn and fiddle with a pencil and gaze out the window, or glance at the clock, when the teacher begins to read a story and it is about a boy.

But because he has a mind, and an imagination—because all kids do, all humans do—he begins to see himself in the fictional boy. Something feels familiar. The boy in the story is scared. He's worried about what is going to happen to him. His parents don't seem to care. But the boy, the fictional boy, Jonas, senses that something is wrong in his world.

Well, the boy in the classroom, the one slouched in his desk, is scared, too. His own world sucks. His own parents—assuming he has them in his life—do their best but are not a source of wisdom or comfort. He hasn't a clue what his own future holds. He suspects it holds nothing. He begins to listen to the story about the scared, uncertain boy. Then the boy in the book meets a man. This is part of the structure of myth, of course. The hero encounters a mentor—often it is someone with magical powers. Jonas, in the book, has this experience. He meets a man who has amazing powers and who is able to give him something intangible, something mysterious, not yet explainable. The boy in the classroom, listening, maybe less restless, attentive by now, knows in his heart that he is not going to have an opportunity to meet a bearded man who will be his mentor. Maybe there have been people in his past—a Cub Scout leader once, a Little League coach, maybe, who tried—but there had been no connection for him; they tried to make him conform, to follow their rules, and it didn't work for him, and he dropped out and drifted away.

But something is happening that he is unaware of. He has met a teacher who is magically transferring excitement to him, and a sense of wonder. So we have a boy who is himself a Jonas. He is a mythic hero, a young boy caught in a world that offers him little, that is in many ways a sick society; and through a mentor—a teacher—a Giver—he begins to undertake his own journey, as Jonas does.

There are other stock situations in myth. There is a threshold that the hero must cross in order to enter the unknown. Jonas gets on a bike and crosses a bridge on his way to Elsewhere. The young boy in South Carolina picks up a telephone on a snowy day. Myth requires a journey. They both set out. Myth requires that they encounter obstacles, entertain doubts, that they despair and feel all is lost. We know, those of us who know *The Giver*, that Jonas experiences all of those things.

We don't know the boy in South Carolina. But we know the rural south. We know our culture. We know what the world offers a semieducated, disaffected boy like him. And so we know that he, too, is going to experience crushing defeats and terrible despair. But for now, during two weeks in February, he makes that mythic journey with a fictional character. There is a moment when Jonas feels like giving up, like giving in.

> He got off [the bicycle] and let it drop sideways into the snow. For a moment he thought how easy it would be to drop beside it himself, to let himself and Gabriel slide into the softness of snow, the darkness of night, the warm comfort of sleep.

But the trials that a mythic hero undergoes test him and reveal his true nature. So it is, with Jonas.

> He pressed his hands into Gabriel's back and tried to remember sunshine. For a moment it seemed that nothing came to him, that his power was completely gone. Then it flickered suddenly, and he felt tiny tongues of

heat begin to creep across and into his frozen feet and legs. He felt his face begin to glow and the tense, cold skin of his arms and hands relax. For a fleeting second he felt that he wanted to keep it for himself, to let himself bathe in sunlight, unburdened by anything or anyone else

But the moment passed and was followed by an urge, a need, a passionate yearning to share the warmth with the one person left for him to love.

And of course his true nature is courageous and unselfish. He becomes, after passing through the trials, like all mythic heroes, transcendent. Maybe, briefly, to the boy in South Carolina, reaching a destination seems possible.

I think the reason the book remains, after all these years, a bestseller (I began writing this on a Wednesday. Now it is Friday. I just checked Amazon again, Today it is #474 . . . up a hundred notches in two days.) is because everywhere—in China and Hungary and Germany and Serbo-Croatia and every one of the twenty-two countries in which this book is published now—readers live in a world that is wounded and needs saving. They want to make that mythic journey with a boy named Jonas. They want to share his passionate yearning and to emerge into a place where there is music.

They want to know it is possible. . . .

When a young reader—whatever age: ten or twelve or fourteen—is captured by a book, is enthralled with a plot and in love with a character, he (or she), curled in a chair, or listening to the voice of a teacher, puts himself into that fictional situation and weighs the choices the fictional character makes, that reader becomes that character for a period of time.

Books for young people have tremendous power over their audience. We're fortunate, in this country, that we have so many wonderful writers for children, so many wonderful librarians, so many wonderful teachers, who understand that power and who use it with wisdom and intelligence. And all we writers do, really, is, as Nemerov said, "say the visible"—the concrete, the details, the things that make a book come to life, that tell the story, that capture the attention, that invite the reader to make a journey. And then, when it works, it does what the poet said: it brings invisibles to view. The invisibles are those abstract, mythic things we care about: integrity, honesty, a sense of history, a hope of future. We try to make them accessible to the young. Interesting to the young. Important to the young.

I look with awe at the list of previous recipients of this award. I'm very honored to be among them. But you know what makes me feel truly honored, truly successful? Knowing that on snowy afternoon in an impoverished home in South Carolina, one troubled, angry boy crossed a threshold when he picked up a telephone, called his eighth grade teacher, and said, with passionate yearning in his voice, "You gotta read to me."

Thank you.

Jacqueline Woodson, 2006 Margaret A. Edwards Award

Honoring the authors who inspired her, Jacqueline Woodson speaks eloquently about her growth as a writer in her acceptance speech for the 2006 Margaret A. Edwards Award.

When I was in fifth grade, I used to stand in front of the bathroom mirror, holding a hairbrush as a microphone and practice giving my speech for the Pulitzer Prize. I didn't really know what the Pulitzer was but had read about a writer getting it in the *Daily News*. The idea that someone could write a book that would not only be read by *strangers* but awarded a *prize*, fascinated me. And the idea that there was actually this award out there for writing was amazing. I had seen the gold and silver stickers on paperbacks in my classroom, but those stickers (which I would later learn were called Newbery) had never been explained to me. The books landed in our classroom—secondhand and already battered. My teachers always seemed excited by these stickered books and encouraged us to read them, but early on I was a cover girl—checking out the covers of books. If the illustration didn't speak to me, I looked no further. Often I was simply looking for people who looked like me and rarely found them.

But the Pulitzer—that made sense. The *Daily News* had said so. The Pulitzer was an award some people somewhere had given to some writer somewhere and the news was big enough for Brooklyn's favorite tabloid to report. I wanted that prize because I because I wanted to write. I must have had this idea that if you got an award, it meant you had written a book. And more than anything, I wanted to one day write a book. But first, I had to practice my Thank-You speech. So many mornings, I stood in our tiny downstairs bathroom and did just that—thanking my grandmother for making me read and making sure I spoke well. Thanking our three cats, Sweetie, Friskie, and Charles. Depending on the day, my brothers and sister might get an acknowledgement, but most of the time, when I was receiving this award, I was an only child. I spoke of the award-winning book, how I had cried during the writing of it. I spoke of my exhaustion in the end. How worth it the struggle was. I sometimes mentioned the Black Panthers—because it was the '70s after all. When I did, I punctuated my appreciation of Angela Davis by raising my own fist into the air.

By the time I was in fifth grade, my favorite uncle had converted to the Nation of Islam and convinced the whole family that eating pork was wrong. He said that the iridescence on ham was the part of the pig that couldn't be killed and that if we ate it, we would eventually die. During the course of my speech, I thanked my uncle for saving my life. I thanked my relatives in South Carolina for the stories they told one another that I wasn't supposed to hear about injustices against various members of the African-American population. I thanked my best friend Maria and her parents for their welcoming me into their Puerto Rican family.

It was a time of race pride when every preadolescent T-shirt in my neighborhood read "Kiss Me, I'm Black" or "Kiss Me, I'm Puerto Rican" and every posted spouted BLACK IS BEAUTIFUL, FREE ANGELA, and BORIQUA FOREVER. Where kids moved through the streets singing "To Be Young, Gifted and Black" and "En Mi Viejo San Juan" at the top of their lungs and danced to the music of the Jackson Five, James Brown, and Aretha Franklin. It was a time when the summers meant double-dutch and hopscotch in the streets and dusk always came too quickly. It was a place where mothers called from high-up windows, beckoning their children home. Standing in the mirror, I didn't know to thank this world—the world that would give me my stories.

Because a part of me never believed I'd really ever get a chance to. A part of me, even as I gave this speech, knew I would never write a book, get an award, stand in front of huge audiences to speak of my appreciation. At ten, the world had already convinced me that I did not have a story. And even if I did, I didn't have a right to tell it.

I don't know how I existed in these parallel worlds—the world of believing and not believing. I didn't know any other writers. I didn't even know, at the age of ten, that black women wrote books. At ten, what I knew for sure was that I was a black girl growing up in Brooklyn who wanted to one day be a writer. And I knew even as I held the hairbrush to my lips, that, in the words of Joe Darion, I was dreaming the impossible dream ["The Impossible Dream," from *Man of La Mancha*]. What black child in New York didn't know every word to that song by the time they were able to do long division? . . . .

And like the other things, we knew everything and nothing about the song. If asked, we would have probably said it was a spiritual written by slaves. We knew it was our people, that it was a song hammered into our heads from kindergarten graduation through high school, that there was always one gifted kid who sang most of it well but always hit at least one bad note.

We thought it was written for us.

And why shouldn't we have? Every single one of us was being told to uplift the race, keep our eyes on the prize, make a way out of no way, do something with our lives. Every single one of us had a grandmother or great aunt or granddaddy who had walked six miles a day to a one-room schoolhouse with no shoes to wear—and the telling always ended with, "So I know you can figure out this here multiplication, spelling, geography, etc." As if their daily trek had some direct connection to our academic ability. Of course we should dream the impossible dream. But before we did that, we had to graduate and get a full time job!

Somewhere during the course of that year, I discovered the works of Mildred Taylor and Virginia Hamilton, of James Baldwin and Toni Morrison. And the world suddenly began to fall in place for me. There is an amazing song by Bernice Johnson Reagon that I've heard performed by Sweet Honey In the Rock called "I Remember, I Believe." . . . When I discovered the song, as an adult, it explained a lot for me—how I could believe while not believing. How I could have hope that one day I would write. How I could hear the voices of both support and dissension and use those voices to fuel a growing urgency.

In my time on this earth as a writer, I've seen a number of amazing people move on to the next place—from Audre Lorde to Virginia Hamilton, from Octavia Butler to Katherine Dunham. But before they moved on, each taught me something about my time here. Most recently, Katherine Dunham, who, in 1992 at the age of 82 began a 47-day fast to protest the United States' deportations of Haitian boat refugees. After a lifetime of work as a dancer, choreographer, writer, and activist, Dunham taught me the importance of keeping on—no matter how old I got, not matter how the times and the work that needed to be done changed.

Audre Lorde, who in writing openly about her battle with cancer during a time when talking about cancer was considered taboo, who in being out and a mom and an activist and a feminist, taught me the importance of being all of these things, of not letting the world silence me, who in writing "your silence will not protect you" taught me the importance of my own voice in the world.

Virginia Hamilton, who I read as a child and met as a young writer, becoming, along with her husband Arnold Adoff, some of the first living hands on my back—always taking the time to teach me, to nurture me, to help me keep on.

Octavia Butler, who under the guise of writing what the world wanted to call science fiction, wrote about feminism and racism and the importance of really looking at the world—watching what it is becoming and taking action.

Each of these women taught me the most important lesson: To do the work that needs to be done, while I'm here. To write with an urgency, a Right Now in my words while I can, for as long as I can, as well as I can. To not forget the people who came before me and those who are coming behind me. To not live this gift of a life in vain. To walk through this world with my eyes wide open. And when I am afraid—because yes, sometimes I am very afraid—to not let the fear silence me. There will be time for silence. But for me, as a writer who is living, who still has so many things I want to say, now is not that time.

While I'm here. Because I won't always be here and sometimes I get so tired of giving my hands to the struggle. Sometimes, I want to just sit down and not think and not question and not feel compelled to act. Some mornings I pick up my pen and ask myself, "Now what?" When the towers came down—now what? When every sign on the subway reminded me to be afraid of brown paper bags—now what? When the front page top of the fold story in the *New York Times* talked about the struggle African-American men still deal with because of racism—now what? When I feel invisible and powerless—now what? And on the days when the voices in my head grow silent, when the world seems to be holding its breath for the next thing, when I stare at the shelves of books I've written and struggle to believe they've made any difference anywhere . . . And then I remember, the child in the mirror who held the hairbrush in her hand . . .

I remember. And I believe.

Since the phone call came on that cold day in January, people have been asking me, "How does it feel?" How does it feel to be awarded for a lifetime achievement? How does it feel to know there are people out there who think your work really matters? How does it feel to write? . . . To write this talk? . . . To write this talk, which will be given in New Orleans . . . in June . . . months after Hurricane Katrina tried to wash this town away? And for months, I've been giving the only answer I know how to give. It feels surreal. As surreal as the writing itself—the way the characters have always come to me, told their stories. The way the stories have always moved through my brain and down to my hand.

In the words of Joan Didion, "Life changes fast. Life changes in the instant." A war begins and rages just outside of our gaze, our friends get sick, babies are born, in the distance there are car horns and sirens and church bells. I leave my house with a new book under my arm a little dazed by its origin . . . Surreal how this world and this life goes on around us. Impossible to take it in and not breathe it back out into a story.

I am honored and flattered to be receiving this award. Margaret Edwards put books in a cart and rode a horse and buggy around town delivering those books to young people. She was outspoken and believed in the power of literature—its ability to change the world. She believed in teenagers and the power of their voices, the importance of introducing them to people they might not have otherwise met and places they would never have seen. I would have loved to have sat down at a table with her and talked about her world. I would have wanted to hear her stories, what injustices in the world informed her actions. What living in a small West Texas town meant for a young girl who was already walking through the world with her eyes wide open.

But we would never meet physically. We were separated by time. We were separated by race. We were separated by geography. Still, our paths crossed, we connected and we are here together this afternoon. I believe time does this—connects us. While I'm here, I hope to connect to as many people as I possibly can. I hope to write books that continue to speak to those who can't speak, who have not yet learned their own power, who the world may try to silence. I want my child and all children to know their voice in the world, to know their power, to remember one of the first lessons they learn as toddlers: "Use your words."

Some kids sing in the mirror. Others practice jokes or their cover-girl smiles. I talked about writing. I talked about the books I'd written, and the books I planned to write some day. I went on and on until someone banged on the door and hurried me off to school. There was so much I didn't know . . . I didn't know the first thing about publishing a book. I didn't know about people behind the book and behind you. I didn't know awards came via phone calls and sometimes even had a check or a cool sticker or plaque accompanying them. I didn't know they started with just one book and someone reading that book—an editor maybe—the way Wendy Lamb first read *Last Summer with Maizon*, who maybe saw something in the writing and in the writer and said, "Nothing you can do is wrong." So that suddenly you had license to write about all the things you'd always dreamed of writing about—about the people you loved and the injustices in the world, and the questions you had—all the *Whys* that were stories inside you. That were there waiting to be written as your ten-year-old eyes watched your own mouth move around words about an award you knew nothing about.

Some of you may know this but many probably don't: One of my first author visits was to an amazing library in Baltimore. I was 25 years old and my first novel, *Last Summer with Maizon*, had been published by Bantam Double-day Dell. I was incredibly wide-eyed and incredibly shy and stunned that I'd been invited all the way to Baltimore to speak about a book few people knew anything about. The library of course was the Enoch Pratt Library. The librarian who invited me was Debbie Taylor. That was a long time ago. And each time something good happened for me after that, Debbie Taylor was always somewhere in the wings. Even recently, when *School Library Journal* wrote about me and this award, it was Debbie who called to say, "I'll be doing the interview." Thank you, Debbie. My new nickname in Brooklyn is Cover Girl. My brother called from Pennsylvania to say, "Someone told me you were a centerfold in Redbook." It goes as it goes.

But nothing happens in a void. If my first editor Wendy Lamb hadn't said to me, "Nothing you can write is wrong," I probably never would have written *Dear One* or *I Hadn't Meant to Tell You This* or *Lena*. When I said to her, "you mean I can write about this stuff in children's books?" she said, "Of course you can." And I have never looked back.

When I was 22, I met Dylis Evans at a party at her house on Long Island. I remember her giving me this bell and telling me to ring it whenever I wanted a publisher to call. I still have the bell. It sits high up on my bookshelf stuffed with tissue paper. No one is allowed to touch it because it was given to me 20-something books ago and I know for a fact that it works! It was Dylis who introduced me to Dianne Hess who would later edit *From the Notebooks of Melanin Sun*.

I remember having a meeting at Scholastic to talk about the many issues in *Melanin Sun*. The thinking was that the book was a bit too bogged down with all that was going on it in—a mom coming out, the homophobia in the community, a fatherless boy who was very short and kept "notebooks," a white girlfriend. I agreed; there was a lot going on. I decided some changes needed to be made. So I made *Melanin Sun* taller, folded my arms, and refused to change anything else. I'm sure I got called a brat more times than I care to know about.

And of course I was afraid to tackle the subject of queerness in a book for young people at a publishing house that didn't have a history of publishing books that dealt with this issue. But I couldn't not write *From the Notebooks of Melanin Sun*. I couldn't let my fear silence me.

Then Nancy Paulsen came along, and with her stories that I didn't even know I had inside of me began to take shape on the page. It's amazing how the writer/editor thing works. I won't go into lots of detail because even with all of these years of writing behind me I still don't quite understand—a curtain gets pulled back, a light shines in. That light is your editor and what is illumined is the story that was always inside of you waiting to be born. And in the fragile embryonic stages of the story, you struggle, you doubt. But with each revision, you and the story grow stronger—and it's the editor that shows you that strength. So I am grateful to each of my editors who have been those lights over the years.

And I am grateful to the librarians who have come up to me—even when I was signing next to, say, Eric Carle, whose line stretched around the Exhibit Hall, while mine consisted of the people stopping by to ask me what was free on my table. I am grateful for the librarians who knew me when and sent me cards and let me sleep in their guestrooms and invited me to their schools and into their university classrooms—you know who you are. You knew me when . . . this when and the whens that have come before this day. I do remember how you believed.

And of course I am grateful to every marketing and publicity person I've ever worked with who did everything from making sure I didn't walk into a crowd with the poppy seeds still in my teeth to being everywhere I needed you to be. How do you do that and always look so clean and awake, even when you've worked until 2:00 a.m.?

And every young reader who has crossed lines of race and class and gender to imagine their feet in another person's shoes.

And I am grateful to the writers who came before me and the ones who walk this world with me, and the ones who are coming behind us. Each story on the page, each poem, every essay is a breath in the world.

I am grateful to my family—my amazing and beautiful family. My partner, Juliet who—yay!—just this month finished her medical residency, and, even with a stack of medical books to read on her beside table, took time to read draft after draft of my novels, always giving amazing feedback too often on only a few hours of sleep—and sometimes with our child in one arm, my manuscript in the other hand, and a friend calling with a medical issue at the other end of the phone. I don't even try to imagine where I'd be without my family.

Which brings me to the child—Toshi—thank you for staying in my belly an extra two weeks so that I could get the final draft of *Locomotion* finished and write most of *Behind You*. If you had been born a week earlier, I might not even be standing here! I know you don't really understand it right now, but this really is better than a playdate.

And I am grateful to my other family—An Na—student, teacher, and friend whose new book, *Wait for Me* is nothing short of stunning and who with her husband James and daughter Juna have been daily lights in my life.

My friend, Toshi Reagon, who when I asked her what I should write my Margaret Edwards speech about said, "You ain't gone yet so write about still being here! Write it for those who can no longer write it." And so I did.

And of course, my agent, Charlotte Sheedy, who couldn't be here because she's recovering from knee surgery. But wow. In the words of Kevin Henkes' Lily, all I can say is Wow!

And, finally, yes finally, with grace, humility and big love, I am grateful to the Margaret Edwards Committee for giving me the chance to dream the impossible dream. For putting the hairbrush back into my hand.

Francesca Lia Block, 2005 Margaret A. Edwards Award

The profound influence of supportive family, colleagues, and friends is a theme in Francesca Lia Block's 2005 Margaret A. Edwards acceptance speech.

The first thing I want to do is thank you. Thank you for being there every day with the books. For reading the books, selecting the books, putting the books into the hands of people who need them. The books that not only bring knowledge, joy, catharsis, but the books that actually transform, the books that save lives. And thank you, Margaret A. Edwards award committee, for choosing my books. By choosing them you are validating a different America. This America believes in fairies (both kinds). This America has stayed up late, crying and making collages with lace and rose petals while people are dying overseas. This America has had her heart broken so many times that it feels like litter in her chest; this is just the latest of her many metaphors. This America still emails her friends poems about it instead of remaining silent. This America is not about greed and violence but about acceptance, love and the healing power of art.

I am going to tell you a story about these things.

I was born, like Weetzie Bat, at the Kaiser on Sunset Boulevard in Hollywood. My first memories are of the house where I lived with my parents and half-brother—a cottage not unlike Grandma Fifi's with sunny windows and a lemon tree in the backyard. My father used to hold me on top of the piano, which I would play with my toes. When I was two we moved to the valley, at the base of Laurel Canyon. That slight distance from the Hollywood I write about so frequently gave it an allure it might not have had if I grew up in its center. Even as a child, I spent a lot of time driving in my parent's Volvo through the green winding canyon filled with crumbling mansions, amaryllis and stained glass. We went to the La Brea tar pits where a sculpture of a mastodon family depicted the mother sinking into the sticky black pool while the father and baby grieved from the shore, the Los Angeles County Museum where mimes entertained in the courtyard, Kiddy Land with its pony rides (like Weetzie, I hated to whip the ponies to make them go) and Griffith Park with its haunted carousel, ferny glades and wading pools. At home, I made magic lands with mud, water, and passionflowers in the backyard or walked in circles, twirling my hair, sucking my lip and telling myself stories out loud. If I got stuck on a plot I obsessively made myself start all over from the beginning. My mother was my best companion. She was always ready to play dolls, gypsies, or Japanese tea party with me. My father, a painter, let me share his art supplies and we spent hours drawing together. Every week he went to a movie studio that artists rented to sketch nude models. Once he brought home some costumes that were being thrown away—an eerie clear plastic cherub mask, a feather boa, a torn rubber monster head, wings, and a glittery black sequin headdress. On Halloween he made a haunted house in his backyard studio, decorating it with his artist's skeleton and skull, as well as the masks and creepy white plaster models of an arm and a hand. These are some of the strongest impressions that color my work.

Of course, one of the hugest influences on my work were the books my parents read to me. When my mom was pregnant my dad read poetry from Keats, Yeats, Dylan Thomas and Pablo Neruda to her swelling belly. As I grew up he told me Greek myths like the *Odyssey* as bedtime stories and revealed that in his previous career as a Hollywood writer he had based his scripts on Shakespeare's plays. Here are a few of the books I cherished most: *Mr. Rabbit and the Lovely Present* by Charlotte Zolotow captured my imagination and heart with Maurice Sendak's lush watercolor illustrations and it's story of finding the perfect expression of love with the help of a kind hearted surreal friend. When I recently re-read *The Animal Family* by Randall Jarrell I saw that I kept retelling the story in that book—an unusual group of individuals, some of them mystical or animal, meet, love each other and form their own family as a way to combat the demon of loneliness that threatens to take us all and may ultimately have another name—death. Some of those elements also appear in another of my favorite books—*The Doll's House* by Rumor Godden in which a family of dolls are rejected by their owners for an ice queen china doll named Marchpane until the ethereal cracker box mama doll Birdy catches on fire from the real birthday candle in the doll-sized lantern. Books like these were as much my friends as the dolls I named Tata, Plunk, Leetie Doll and Picnic Rose, the stuffed bear family that lived in my doll house and my dog Teddy Dradle, a curly white cockapoo who followed me wherever I went. ["I still have Piggy—rubbed so long he's just a wooden ball with tiny stick legs!" heart]

As I grew older, music and dancing joined books as a way to deal with feelings of loneliness or disconnection in the world. I fell madly in love with Cat Stevens and spent hours dancing to his music while my patient father shone a desk lamp to make a spot light for me. I also adored Joni Mitchell and was fascinated with the idea of poetry that could make you dance. Early on, I had a dream of writing books that affected people in as visceral way as music did. In my rebellious teenage phase I discovered punk with its hard edge. The sweat of that music even made me more aware of my desire to move people physically with my art. My best friend, Dirk's prototype, Geoff, picked me up in his 1965 Mustang convertible, we drank expensive white wine he'd stolen from his single mom's wine cellar and drove through Laurel Canyon to see bands like X, the Go-Go's and the Cramps at the Roxy or the Whiskey a Go Go. Those nights had such a different quality from the sweetness of my early childhood. I remember waiting in front of my house for Geoff, standing near the prickly, heat-soaked, red-blossoming, deadly oleander bushes, trying out my first (and last) cigarette in a fake ivory and pink rhinestone cigarette holder, listening to the owls in the trees and seeing a bat fly out of the gulley across the way. That was a quintessential moment. Darkness was encroaching upon me. My father had been diagnosed with cancer, I was about to go away to Berkeley for college, I was drinking too much and terrified. Luckily, I had my stories. I had begun to make up little ones about a girl named Weetzie Bat with a bleach blonde flat top who wore engineer boots with '50's prom dresses, surfed and slammed at punk clubs. As you may know, the name came from the license plate on a pink pinto that I saw on the freeway one day with a blonde pixie at the wheel. Weetzie. I wonder where the real one is now, and if she has ever seen my books. I'd like to thank her. The Weetzie of those early stories was very shrill, a little harsh and one-dimensional, a cartoon character who I sketched in profile with her upturned nose and Harlequin glasses.

While studying English Literature at UC Berkeley I developed her more and more. As I walked home through the quiet, blossomy hills of North Berkeley I made up stories about her to soothe and entertain myself. I knew I wanted to be a serious author someday (I had won a short fiction and poetry award) but I didn't think that these stories were the way I would enter that world. They were purely expressions of love, an ode to Los Angeles and the family and friends I yearned for.

One still-dark dawn my phone rang. I heard my mom's voice and knew what had happened. I flew back to L.A. My father had died. The last time I had seen him was Valentine's weekend. We had gone to an anti-war protest where we had danced to a band and then eaten sushi together.

For those of you who have read my book *Echo*, the part where Echo and her mother, Eva, see a white horse after Caliban's death is from an actual experience my mom and I had with a horse when my dad died.

> When she looked up the white horse was standing there as if the fog had taken this shape. His muscled, moon-silver body. His toss of mane and tail. The long shivery slope of his nose. She moved toward him as slowly as possible, holding her breath. In the dreamtime she didn't question how he could be here; all she knew was that she needed to touch him. She put out her hand and he hesitated, a tremor passing through both of them, before he reached out and nuzzled her. He was warm and she felt the delicate jets of the breath through tremulous nostrils, the bristling hairs, the hard strength of teeth beneath the furl of his lip. His eyes were what made her know. The big dark brown tender light-filled orbs that were the eyes of Caliban.
>
> Psycho pomp. Spirit guide.

A few days later I went back to Berkeley for my graduation. I was walking along Telegraph Avenue when I saw something on the ground. I was drawn to pick it up, in spite of the dirty pavement on which it lay. It was a small white plastic horse with a green plastic cowboy rider. Whether this was a message from my father or just something that I chose to interpret that way really doesn't matter. I felt a profound comfort and connection at this time. That is one of the wonders of the imagination. It can heal us so much, just sparked by a little piece of plastic.

My father had mailed a letter to me the day he died so I received it from my Berkeley mailbox after he was gone. It read, "Live without guilt. Let happiness be your closest friend." These were the words he left me with.

I think that in his way, he was trying to tell me to live in love and without fear. I can't say he did that in his life, but I know it was his intention. My father never read WEETZIE BAT but his spirit fills the pages, especially these final ones:

> When they got home, it was a purple, smoggy L.A. twilight. Weetzie and My Secret Agent Lover Man and Cherokee and Witch Baby and Slinkster Dog and Go-Go Girl and the puppies Pee Wee, Wee Wee, Teenie Wee, Tiki Tee, and Tee Pee were waiting on the front porch drinking lemonade and listening to Iggy Popp's "Lust for Life" as the sky darkened and the barbecue summer smells filled the air.
>
> Weetzie ran up to them first and flung her arms around Duck and then Dirk. Then all six of them held on to one another in a football huddle and the dogs slunk around their feet.

That night they all ate linguini and clam sauce that My Secret Agent Lover Man made, and they drank wine and lit the candles.

Weetzie looked around at everyone—she saw Dirk, tired, unshaven, his hair a mess; he hardly ever looked like this. But his eyes shone wet with love. Duck looked older, there were lines in his face she hadn't remembered seeing before, but he leaned against Dirk like a little boy. Weetzie looked at My Secret Agent Lover Man finishing his linguini, sucking it up with his pouty lips. Cherokee was pulling on his sleeve and he leaned over and kissed her and then put her onto his lap to help him finish that last bite of pasta. Witch Baby sat alone, mysterious and beautiful.

Weetzie's heart felt so full with love, so full, as if it could hardly fit in her chest. She knew that they were all afraid. But love and disease are both like electricity, Weetzie thought. They are always there—you can't see or smell or hear, touch or taste them, but you know they are there like a current in the air. We can choose, Weetzie thought, we can choose to plug into the love current instead. And she looked around the table at Dirk and Duck and My Secret Agent Lover Man and Cherokee and Witch Baby— all of them lit up and golden like a wreath of lights.

I don't know about happily ever after... but I know about happily, Weetzie Bat thought.

My father's death took away any last fantasy of happily ever after but his life taught me about happily.

I moved back to L.A. and got a job at a clothing store on Melrose and (like Echo) at the art gallery where my father had shown his paintings. His work still hangs on the walls of my home today—oil or watercolor still lives of flowers and fruits that have a completely transcendent quality. The way he imbued everyday objects with such spirituality, or perhaps just perceived it in them, taught me how to attempt to do the same thing with words.

One day I was working at the gallery when I got a phone call from my friend Kathryn Jacobi, an artist and illustrator who had handed on my manuscript of *Weetzie Bat* to her editor Charlotte Zolotow and Joanna Cotler who was an editor working for Charlotte at that time. When she told me they wanted to publish it I began to weep. Do you know when you have a deep desire? It feels imperative that it be fulfilled or you will not be complete. This is different from something you want. It is a need, an innate longing toward something that feels inevitable, even when you are filled with doubt that it may not occur. I had always had this knowing about becoming a writer. I am blessed that this desire was fulfilled, especially at such a young age and in such a miraculous way.

It is interesting to me that just a few months before I heard that my book was to be published, I met my future boyfriend who asked me what I did. I told him, "I'm a writer." Of course, I hadn't had anything published but I suddenly had the chutzpah to make this pronouncement. I believe that this confidence and intention really helped bring about this miracle. For some reason, probably because of my parents' nurturing, I always have had more faith in myself as a writer than in any other aspect of my life. I don't suffer from writer's block and the demons in my head aren't critical of my work. However, they are critical of me in other ways. I try to use my healthier writer mindset as a model and apply it to other aspects of my life because it seems that if we have faith within (or love, or wholeness) it will be reflected without and come back to us.

Sometimes my writer's mind knows the answer even if I'm not able to live it in my daily life. In *Missing Angel Juan*, Witch Baby needs to learn to release her grip on her beloved in order to truly grow and love herself.

> Dear Angel Juan,
>
> Do you know when they say soul-mates? Everybody uses it in personal ads. "Soul mate wanted." It doesn't mean too much now. But soul-mates—think about it. When your soul—whatever that is anyway—something so alive when you make music or love and so mysteriously hidden most of the rest of the time, so colorful and big but without color or shape—when your soul finds another soul it can recognize even before the rest of you knows about it. The rest of you just feels sweaty and jumpy at first. And your souls get married without even meaning to—even if you can't be together for some reason in real life, your souls just go ahead and make the wedding plans. A soul's wedding must be too beautiful to even look at. It must be blinding. It must be like all the weddings in the world—gondolas with canopies of doves, champagne glasses shattering, wings of veils, drums beating, flutes and trumpets, showers of roses. And after that happens you know—that's it, this is it. But sometimes you have to let that person go. When you're little, people, movies and fairy tales all tell you that one day you're going to meet this person. So you keep waiting and it's a lot harder than they make it sound. Then you meet and you think, okay, now we can just get on with it, but you find out that sometimes your soul brother partner lover has other ideas about that. They want to go to New York and write their own songs or whatever. They feel like you don't really love them but the idea of them, the dream you've had since you were a kid about a panther boy to carry you out of the forest of your fear or an angel to make love and celestial music with in the clouds or a genie twin to sleep with you inside a lamp. Which doesn't mean they're not the one. It just means you've got to do whatever you have to do for you alone. You've got to believe in your magic and face right up to the mean nasty part of yourself that wants to keep the one you love locked up in a place in you where

no one else can touch them or even see them. Just the way when somebody you love dies you don't stop loving them but you don't lock up their
souls inside you. You turn that love into something else, give it to somebody else. And sometimes in a weird way when you do that you get closer
than ever to the person who dies or the one your soul married.

Like Witch Baby, over the next few years I struggled with painful love relationships, with being alone, depression. My stress manifested as physical illness.
Although I could write about letting go, I couldn't always do it. But I always
had my writing, and I had faith in myself as a writer. And I had my amazing
mother, Gilda, and two of the best editors in the world, Charlotte Zolotow and
Joanna Cotler, to nurture and support me. They accepted me, and so, more and
more, I accepted myself.

Charlotte with her soft voice, her soft hair, her brilliant blue eyes and crys-
talline mind. She said, "I see more here," about *Weetzie*, and, subsequently, five
sequels emerged over the years. She could say one or two words and the whole
point of the book would come into focus, so that I could bring across that truth
to my reader and learn it myself. In the case of *Witch Baby*, she did more than
give me a few words. She basically reworked the entire structure of that book and
in the process taught me so much about writing. Charlotte is so brave. Brave to
publish a book about a boy who loves a doll and a book about death for children.
These in a climate where she received shocked responses from people because
the rabbit in *Mr. Rabbit and the Lovely Present* was not wearing pants! Brave to
discover and publish *Weetzie Bat*. Brave to keep writing the books that make me
cry when I read them to my children, even though she is struggling with physical
hardships. I have called her my fairy godmother many times and there is still
no better description of her role in my life. *Weetzie Bat* was a pumpkin that she
turned into a chariot to take me to new worlds. It was a mouse that became a
horse, a ragged dress that became a gown, and, most of all, a glass slipper which
has made it possible for me to dance into my career as a writer. When discovered
by others it was the glass slipper that brought love to my door, into my life.

What about Joanna? Joanna Cotler is not only my editor of eighteen years—
she is also my sister. How many people can say that about the person they work
with, the one who can okay a project and send a check to pay rent and feed
their kids and buy cute shoes just for doing what they love best. When I work
on a book with Joanna I experience a profound healing. We not only talk about
the project at hand, but we speak about our personal lives and I always come
away with enlightenment about the work and about myself. We speak in half-
sentences and fragments, understanding each other's thoughts before we are finished expressing them. We laugh hysterically at things someone eavesdropping
would probably never understand and we cry together, too. We get mad at each

other like siblings and we trust the love between us in this same way. She sings to my crying children over the phone, sends me flowers, talks about dance, art and poetry and comforts me when my heart is broken. Joanna is changing the world. She is a powerful force. She is making everything possible for me. I love her so much that I really can't come up with the right metaphor and I am usually pretty good with that.

One reason that Joanna has been able to do so many life-changing things for me, and for so many, is because of the people around her. Bill Morris with his elfin face, sly eyes, sharp wit and heartfelt appreciation for librarians was a force in publishing that will always be remembered. Patty Campbell and Michael Cart acknowledged what I was doing before almost anyone and heralded my work with a passion for which I am most grateful. I am thankful for everyone on the team. Susan Katz and HarperCollins for their ongoing support, YALSA, *School Library Journal* and Lillian Gerhardt for initiating the award.

Another person I want to tell you about is my agent Lydia Wills. Lydia, striding around in her amazing shoes, doing cartwheels in them on the street to entertain my children, making deals, making things happen. When we first met she told me about her aunt, a struggling artist who she always wanted to support somehow, even from the time Lydia was a child, and who, she said, reminded her of me. Her passion for her clients is fierce, innate and almost maternal. She operates from a perfect blending of intellect and instinct. Even when she doesn't like an idea I have, or think it's a good career move, she treats it with respect. There is a certain silence on the phone and I know, Lydia is listening. Her mind is working and she will fearlessly find the solution to whatever problem exists.

My mother, Joanna, and Lydia have always supported me in writing the books that my psyche demands I write, rather than trying to steer me in more commercial or safe directions. With their support, I have written and published fantasy (*Ecstsia* and *Primavera*), erotica (*Nymph*) and the non-fiction book about my daughter, *Guarding the Moon*. This last one came about because after she was born I had no interest in anything except her. Lydia and Joanna recognized this and encouraged me to explore it in my writing. Lydia encouraged me to go deep into personal issues about my body that arose during my pregnancy. I might not have had the courage to do this otherwise. Joanna is fearless. She published *The Hanged Man*, a book about incest that inspired a young woman to write me a letter, saying that she had suffered through a similar experience and because of the book was able to speak of it for the first time. Without questioning it, Joanna published *Girl Goddess #9,* in which the first short story is about a three year old and the last about an eighteen year old. *Echo* with its unconventional structure. *Wasteland* and *The Rose and the Beast* with their controversial themes. Most recently, Joanna recognized that my new book *Psyche in a Dress*, the story of a young woman's transformation from one Greek-myth-based character to another as she interacts with a series of damaged men, and her ultimate emergence, might work better as a narrative poem. This brilliant idea made the book suddenly "work" and inspired me to fill it with more transformational imagery to reflect the overall theme within the individual lines. It also honored my lifelong love of poetry. I had studied the modernist poets—H.D. in particular, and Emily Dickinson at U.C. Berkeley—and desired to bring the rhythms, imagism, emotion and nuance of poetry into my work as much as possible.

As Joanna Cotler and Lydia Wills continue to trust my creative process more and more, I, in turn trust it more myself. Simply said, without them I would not have been able to write, much less publish, many of my books.

I have always written about the need to accept others and their differences. It isn't something I am consciously trying to teach in a didactic way; it is just a natural part of my world and so is hopefully conveyed in the stories I am compelled to tell. Because of my nurturing parents, colleagues and friends, I have learned to accept myself as a writer. However, I have not fully accepted myself as a person, as a woman. This has been a long and painful journey, the journey toward self love. But I know it is something I, like all of us, are meant to learn, and hopefully, having experienced the opposite, I will be able to teach it as well. By giving me this award you are not only honoring me as a writer. I feel your love and respect for me as a person, just as I feel love and respect for who you are and what you do.

Recently, I was interviewed for the *L.A. Times Magazine* by Alan Rifkin who was doing a piece on what he calls "Southern California Dream Realism" how so many L.A. writers seem to be having and writing a continuation of the same dream, using elements like the desert, the empty swimming pool, old Hollywood, drugs, ghosts. He asked how my work has been changing, how the dream is evolving. After a good deal of thought I realized that I am more concerned than ever with breaking down boundaries. Between realism and magic, the physical and the spiritual, dark and light, masculine and feminine, age and youth. Respecting the differences, but recognizing the potential for merging.

I believe that by giving me this award you are supporting the dissolution of barriers that separate us from each other. Who knows how much healing can occur in a world where they no longer exist?

I'm going to end by reading the last part of *Necklace of Kisses*, the latest Weetzie Bat book due out in August. Weetzie and her secret agent lover man have just been reunited. Their kiss is a symbol of how love, the greatest boundary dissolver of all, transforms and heals us. How love is really magic and magic, love . . .

> Somewhere in the Pacific Ocean, a mermaid with the legs of a woman swam in a school of dolphins to a cave covered with barnacles. The dolphins whistled good-bye and surged off. The mermaid went into the cave

and found her mother sleeping there in a pile of pearls she had wept.

Esmeralda Escobar woke suddenly in her apartment near downtown Los Angeles and grabbed her sleeping husband's shoulders. "Mira!" she said. He opened his eyes and rubbed them three times to make sure he was not dreaming when he saw the girl he had married, grown older now, sitting beside him, no longer invisible, her horses' mane of black hair loose around her shoulders.

Dirk McDonald and Duck Drake had the same dream: Weetzie had come home. She was standing on the doorstep, naked and laughing. They rolled over in bed, found each other and made love in their canyon house of cherry wood and stained glass windows.

Ping Chong Jah Love felt something fluttering against her face. She woke to see two huge, fluorescent-blue butterflies in her bedroom. The pair circled for a while and then landed on sleeping Valentine Jah-Love's big, bare shoulder, where they began to mate delicately. Ping did not take this as a sign of global warning, or any other planetary distress, but as a sure message that Weetzie and Max had found each other again.

In Santa Barbara, Cherokee Bat woke suddenly, sat at the sewing machine in the shape of a sphinx, and began to sew. She was making a sleeveless cream-silk sheath over slim, sheer cream chiffon pants and a cream raw silk three quarter length coat with a pale blue lining covered with silver stars. In the lining, she would put tiny notes, little charms to honor and protect the enchantress, her mother.

In a café on Telegraph Avenue, Witch Baby sat across the table from her beloved Angel Juan and said, "What were you looking for ?"

"You," he answered.

"But you didn't know it?"

"Not until now."

She nodded. She said, "Now I need to find what I am looking for."

Hilda Doolittle sat at her desk in her one-room Echo Park apartment, looking out over Sunset Boulevard through a window hung with skeleton lights. She was writing a poem called "The Goddess in You." On the wall she saw the unmistakable shadow of a woman, though there was no one there.

A young starlet left the hotel room of the producer with whom she had spent the evening and who was now asleep on the couch. She was carrying a white case covered with roses. She drove away from the pink hotel, never to return. As she merged onto the freeway, her car trunk popped open, the latch on the white case undid itself and a pink and green silk dress flew off into the night sky.

While everyone in the ballroom kissed each other, Heaven stepped onto the balcony. As soon as the moonlight touched Heaven, Haven emerged.

"We need to send her some CDs," said Haven. "She's still talking about 'Seasons in the Sun.'"

Heaven rolled her eyes. They took each other's hands and looked out over the grounds of the pink hotel.

"What a strange and beautiful night," Heaven sighed.

All of the little atrium shops were dark. Except for one.

In her Beautiful World, Lacey was weaving a tapestry telling a story out of her body. It was about people on fire. It was about people in love. It was about people falling from burning buildings. It was about people discovering they could fly.

Ursula Le Guin, 2004 Margaret A. Edwards Award

In her expansive 2004 acceptance speech, Ursula Le Guin talks about creating the fantasy world of Earthsea and the shifting boundaries of YA lit.

THE YOUNG ADULT IN THE YA

If anybody knows what young adult fiction is, it's you—this audience. I feel foolish trying to say anything about it to you. I tried writing vast generalities about young adult fiction and discovered that all I really know is what I do, insofar as I know what that is. The truth is, I just did young adult fiction without thinking about it. And it's very nice to be told by the Margaret Edwards Award that I *did* it satisfactorily. But I still don't know what it was I was doing.

How did I begin doing it? Unexpectedly. Herman Schein of Parnassus Press, who had published my mother's books for young children, wanted to publish books for older kids, and so he asked me to write one—a fantasy. And I said, Oh no, no, I can't do that, I haven't written anything for children, don't know how, quite impossible, thank you very much, and ran away.

And I got home and rued my words. (Nobody can rue words more truly than a writer.) I'd never been asked to write a book. I'd submitted stories and novels for ten years to publishers who hadn't asked for them and didn't want them, and now, a *proposal?* Oh yes, yes! But no: I haven't written for kids, I have no idea what it involves, I don't like thinking about a specific audience, I refuse to put any restrictions on my imagination or vocabulary, and the stuff I want to write about isn't teenage stuff. And a fantasy, he said. Like Tolkien? Oh my heavens! Compete with Shakespeare, sure! Forget it.

But thinking about Tolkien took my mind away to thinking about wizards. . . and so to something that had bothered me about wizards . . . Prospero, Merlin, Gandalf—all old. Peaked hat, white beard. Why? What were they before they were old beardy men? Young men. Smooth cheeks. Kids. How did kids get to be old wizards? By being young wizards, evidently. Learning the craft, going to . . . wizard school?

Huh. Hey. *There's* an idea.

This is not a claim to have invented it. I plant no flags and do not pee on fences. In *The Sword in the Stone* T. H. White has Merlin say something funny about going to wizard school, and I'm sure there are other predecessors. But, in 1968, nobody I knew of had worked the idea out. And it took hold of me like a bulldog. No, more like a boa constrictor—it enwrapped and devoured me. I became it. This is what writing novels is like. Being an elephant living inside a boa constrictor. The Little Prince knew all about it.

The conception was not just of a school of magic, but of a child gifted with an essentially unlimited power who needs—urgently needs—to learn how to know and control such power. That is a big idea. It reverberates. It contains worlds. So, a few months later the elephant emerged from the boa constrictor as *A Wizard of Earthsea*. Herman Schein was happy with it, and his wife Ruth designed its marvelous cover. And I was happy, too—I had a book I knew was something closer to what I'd hoped to write than anything I'd yet written.

I think it was Herman who first said to me, don't worry about the vocabulary and the audience and all that: all a young adult novel has to have is a protagonist over twelve and under twenty. Is there anything else in fact that makes a YA a YA? It sounds like a rhetorical question, but it isn't; I am really asking you. There may be other requirements or rules for the YA novel, and I may have even have followed them in my YA novels. Writers do a great many things of which they are not only unconscious but ignorant. Don't let the naïve fallacy of authorial omnipotence or the critical fallacy of authorial intent fool you for a minute. A book is planned, always, to some extent, and some books are very closely planned; but in writing, we fiction writers work in the dark, perhaps more than any other artists except poets, because we work with language inside the mind. We cannot be thinking about what we write as we write, because we are using the principle tool of thinking, language, to write with—and we have to use it for the writing not for thinking. We cannot be intellectually, articulately conscious of what we're doing as we write any more than we can be intellectually, articulately conscious of the actual process and intent of typing on a keyboard while we type. To think about it consciously, in words, would stop us right there, fingers frozen above the keys. And therefore most fiction writers learn, taoistically, to cherish our ignorance and trust it to do our job. . . . So long as we have been to wizard school. We do have to learn the craft. That's all we have under our control and can use intentionally: craft. We are crafty people. The rest is gift.

Whatever rules I was ignorantly following, then, the *Wizard* came out and was approved as a YA, getting the Boston Globe/Horn Book award, which I hardly knew how to value, back then, and taking my publisher rather by surprise at how it went on selling.

Now, here is an example of intentionality in planning: I had wondered why wizards were always not only white haired, but white men. I wasn't ready yet to question the gender, only the color. The only reason for the whiteness of wizards seemed to be that our fantasy tradition came largely from Northern Europe, with its weird skin-color hang-ups. So I just reversed the convention. My hero and all his people are reddish-brown to black, while the more barbaric or villainous types are white. Some people notice this, many don't. I prefer my subversion to be sneaky, not preachy

That was a deliberate, political decision, made "outside" the writing. Here's an example of the stuff you write while you're just following your story, "ignorantly," without knowing what it implies. A year or so after the Wizard came out, I was pleasantly surprised to discover that it was full of hints of more to come. Right on the first page I had written about

> the man called Sparrowhawk, who in his day became both dragonlord and Archmage. His life is told of in the Deed of Ged and in many songs, but this is a tale of the time before his fame, before the songs were made.

Now I'd thought this was just a crafty trick, learned mostly from Dunsany and Tolkien: the indication of time before the story and time after it and a great geography all around it, which gives the story a chance to reverberate.

But there was more to it than that. I had announced before I even knew who he was that Ged was a dragonlord and the Archmage. When I wrote that sentence I didn't know what an Archmage was, let alone a dragonlord.

So. How did he do that, how did he get there, what did those words mean?

I learned what Archmages and dragonlords were by writing the first book; but Ged himself got there while I wasn't watching. I was in the second book, looking away, looking east to the Kargad Lands, writing about a girl who, like him, had been given a terrible power, but unlike him, wasn't taught rightly how to handle it.

People ask forever, where do you get your ideas from, and I have written several long essays about it and still have no idea where I get my ideas from, except some of them. *The Tombs of Atuan* came directly from a three-day trip to eastern Oregon: the high desert, the high, dry, bony, stony, sagebrush and juniper country, just about as far as you can get from this soggy Florida. It wasn't the first time I'd seen desert, I am a Westerner after all, but it was the first time I had stayed in desert country, heard that silence, walked in twilight on that dangerous, infinitely fragile land. And driving home with the car full of kids and sweat and dust and twigs of sagebrush, I knew I was in love and had a book. The landscape gave it to me. It gave me Tenar and where she lived.

So the Wizard got a sequel, and soon I started the third book. Trilogies were not obligatory back then, let alone series. It was still possible to write one fantasy

novel, or two, and stop. But as I started *The Farthest Shore* I was planning two
more books: one following Ged into middle age, and one following Tenar. And
then stop.

Because my publishers—Atheneum by then—and I thought of the books as
YA, I knew I had to have a young protagonist; but Earthsea had to have a king,
too, so there you are. Young prince meets older wizard and they go sailing off
together into death. Nothing to it.

So having found out what happened to Ged, I started on the fourth book,
the one where I was to find out what happened to Tenar. I wrote a chapter, and
stopped, because I didn't understand what was happening to Tenar. She had given
up magic, she was a farmwife with a couple of kids. What was she thinking of?

It took me seventeen years to find out. During those years, the second wave
of feminism broke, and I learned how to write as myself, from the sensibility
and intellect of a grown woman. That was not the commonest thing in any
genre, even realism, and fantasy had been particularly male-centered. It was a
radical change.

The key to my fourth book of Earthsea was not Tenar herself, but Therru, a
young child who has been terribly used. When I saw that child I had my book.
But Therru is not yet an adolescent, and not even a protagonist, and everybody
else in the story is middle-aged. Where is the obligatory teenager?—I have to
confess I didn't worry about it. I had grown up, my characters had grown up; if
I thought about it I guess I thought, well, I hope my readers have grown up too.
I went ahead and wrote the book I had to write. At the end the king was on his
throne, the lovers were in each other's arms, and my private title for it was
Better Late Than Never. Publicly I called *Tehanu* "the last book of Earthsea"
because I thought it was. Oh, idiot author.

It was met with some shrill accusations of man-hating feminism from people
who think being a hero means you win. But I guess most of my readers had
indeed grown up, because they liked it fine. And I was happy again because I
had brought my tale to its happy ending, ha, ha.

Again, omens and indications in the text, hints of story to come . . . And this
time, to jog my obliviousness, letters from readers: Who is going to be the next
Archmage? Who or what is Tehanu? What are the dragons? And a huge blooper,
which I had already realized with horror and hoped nobody would notice but of
course they did, though they were very kind and tactful about bringing it to my
attention: the Master Summoner in the third book is dead, in the land of the
dead, but in the fourth book he is alive and apparently well on Roke Island. Oh,
idiot idiot author!

Sometimes your mistake is your guide. I'd heard Rusty Schweikert the astro-
naut tell the tale of how when he went outside the space craft to do some external repair he forgot a tool he needed, and while they were getting it to him he

had the first free time he had ever had on the mission: no programmed activity for five whole minutes. Hanging there on his lifeline in space, idle, because of a mistake, because of something he forgot, he had time to look around. And he looked, and he saw the Earth. The Earth his home, immense and fragile, shining there among the stars. A vision that changed his life forever.

That's a beautiful and useful learning story, and I used it. I looked at what I'd got wrong, and saw why it was wrong—because right wasn't quite what I'd thought it was. By way of answering some of the questions I'd caused by absent-mindedly reviving the dead, or had otherwise left unanswered, I wrote the various *Tales of Earthsea*, in which I finally established a coherent history. Certain features which, in 1968, I'd just bought wholesale from the heroic fantasy tradition—such as the supremacy and the celibacy of male wizards—I had to really think about now, and explain, and fit into my Earthsea as I now perceived it, seen not only from the top, from the seats of power, but from below, through the eyes of the powerless, women and children, ordinary people. Some people think this change of view has led to a loss of enchantment in the stories. I don't. The last Tale led me straight into a nest of dragons. Soon after that, I wrote *The Other Wind*, which brings together all those questions: who Tehanu is, who the dragons are, and how, when clever people meddle with it through hubris or through fear, death itself might go wrong.

There are young people in these last two books—Irian/Dragonfly, young Ogion, my dear Kargish Princess—but the books don't obey the teenage protagonist rule, and I don't think they're definably YA. Yet kids as well as adults seem to buy and read them, and I've had no protests so far about the advanced senility of Ged and Tenar. Why are the books thus forgiven? Is it because they're fantasy? Is this a well-known fact, which I have just discovered with cries of Eureka! that fantasy doesn't have to follow the YA rule, because it bridges the gaps between age groups?

We read *Alice in Wonderland* or *The Wind in the Willows* first at eight, or earlier if they're read to us, and again at twelve, maybe, and again maybe every decade or so: and every time we read them we're a different person, yet each time, if we let them do it, they give us what is "appropriate to our age-group"—kiddies or mid-lifers or wrinklies. The *Jungle Books* contain stories that one may read happily at ten, and understand with a hard jolt at forty-five. *The Once and Future King* is as magical, exasperating, fascinating, and moving to me now as it was when it was published. *The Hobbit* doesn't carry across the kid-to-adult gap reliably for everyone, but (going the other direction in Middle Earth) nine-year-olds are now reading *The Lord of the Rings*. Yet *The Lord of the Rings* is a fully adult book about fully adult concerns, with no children in it at all. Short adults, yes. But no kids.

So, the Edmund Wilsons of the world croak, what else is new? Fantasy is *all* infantile. Childish escapism. Mind-mush. Talking animals, elves, bushwa! I was charmed to learn that somebody said of Edmund Wilson that he always thought he was the only grown-up in the room. It is a common delusion of critics. It shouldn't be encouraged, but it can be ignored.

What should not be ignored is the curious capacity fantasy has of satisfying both the child and the adult—and even, and even most particularly, that creature of tormented and insatiable and uncomprehended and infinite needs and longings, the adolescent. How does fantasy do it? Or what does it do that none of the other genres including realism does?

Fantasy is the oldest form of literature. Even if storytelling began with Oog reciting to the family around the fire in the cave the true and factual story of How I Killed a Mammoth, you and I know that Oog's tale was not totally realistic. Elements of fantasy slipped in—the size of the mammoth, the length of the tusks, the intrepidity of Oog . . . It got better every time he told it. And after a couple of generations maybe it was the tale of How Great Hero Father Oog slew the Lord of the Mammoths, which is why we are the People of the Long Tusk—a legend, a myth. A work of the imagination. A fantasy.

They all begin in the same place, the place in our mind that knows what story is. What reality may be, what really happened, we cannot tell; what we can tell is the story, the infinitely flexible, wonderfully rearrangeable, extremely useful story. With it we remake reality. We remake it according to our desires and according to our needs. The truth of story is not fact. Neither is it mere wishful thinking. Story tells human truth, serving human community, and spiritual longing. And the stories that call most on the imagination work on a deep level of the mind, beneath reason (therefore incomprehensible to rationalists), using symbol as poetry does to express what can't be said directly, using imagery to express what can't be perceived directly—using indirection to indicate the truthward direction.

And here myth and imaginative fiction run a risk; all fiction does, but it's particularly destructive to fantasy: the risk of being rationalized—interpreted, reduced to allegory, read as a message. Such reduction is a nefarious act. Teachers and critics indulge in it with the best of motives, but they leave ruin in their wake. Fortunately, the strongest fantasies simply shrug off interpretation like a horse twitching off a fly. Everybody wants to tell us what *Alice in Wonderland* means, and the more they talk about Charles Dodgson and Victorian mores and mathematics and the libido, the farther they get from Lewis Carroll and Alice, who go on about their business on the chess board among the dodos quite intact.

Take the currently almost unquestioned assumption that fantasy concerns a Battle Between Good and Evil. This assumption permits the author to declare one side good and the other bad without further inquiry as to what makes a person or an action good or evil. The heroes and the villains are equally arrogant, competitive, thoughtless, and bloodyminded, and so the Battle goes on till the Problem of Evil is solved in a final orgy of violence and a win for the so-called Good team.

Being akin to legend and folktale and myth, with no necessary allegiance to modernism or realism or any limiting school of fiction, fantasy draws its scenery and characters and images and symbols from the whole range of human story-telling back to quite primitive times, and it doesn't have to clothe its people with distracting realistic trappings and contemporary disguises but can present them quite nakedly—the brave man, the kind woman, the mistreated child, the villain, the king, the traitor, the fool. Character is often less important in fantasy than role (which can also be said of Greek tragedy and much of Shakespeare, where role and character are often the same thing.) To a careless reader such stark stuff may appear to be morally simplistic, black and white. Carelessly written, that's what it is.

But careless reading of genuine fantasy will not only miss nuance, it will miss the whole nature and quality of the work. Fantasy is in fact particularly suited to examining the difference between good and evil, both in act and in intent. The imagination is the instrument of ethics. Imaginative literature offers the opportunity to test motive and behavior, to see how the unconscious may control the seemingly rational, to understand how the bravest deed may leave a track of ruin, to ask what the road to Hell is paved with, and why.

Americans think obsessively in terms of war and battle. It is a suspect metaphor. I don't write about wars between good and evil. What I write about—like most novelists—is people making mistakes, and people—other people or the same people—trying to prevent or correct those mistakes, while inevitably making more mistakes. The "problem of evil" in Earthsea is pretty much what it is here: that people don't or won't recognize the evil they do. In the first book, Ged doesn't know who he is, because he doesn't recognize his own shadow, the shadow we all cast.

Immature people crave and demand moral certainty: this is bad, this is good. Adolescents struggle to find a sure moral foothold in this bewildering world; they long to feel they're on the winning side, or at least a member of the Good team. To them, heroic fantasy may offer a vision of moral clarity. But a battle between unquestioned Good and unexamined Evil is a mere excuse for violence—as brainless, useless, and base as aggressive war in the real world. I hope that teenagers find the real heroic fantasies, like Tolkien's. I know such fantasies continue to be written. They don't have to be written for kids; they'll find them, whoever they're written for.

Which brings me to my final thought about young adult fiction. When I was in my teens, I certainly didn't feel that in order to interest me a book had to be about other adolescents. I got enough of them at school. I wanted to know about being grown up, and novels offered a chance to find out what that was like from inside. Kittens playing are playing cat. So like all reading children who have the chance (which usually means the public library) I read way ahead of myself, blundering into Austen and Voltaire and Dostoyevsky and Dinesen and Dunsany and Steinbeck and Forster and you name it, understanding bits and not understanding lots; but that's how we learn to speak and read, isn't it?—by doing it, not word-by-word-exactly-correct, but with mistakes and misunderstandings, in bits and gulps and clumps that finally begin to stick together and make sense. Literature is a major tool for understanding the world and the life we have to live, and we learn to use it by using it.

The rule that the YA book is about young adults may apply best to the realistic novel of contemporary teenage life and problems, and to historical novels. In other genres, the adolescent reader doesn't seem to demand adolescent protagonists. That all the characters are adult doesn't stop a kid from reading *The Virginian*, or any other good Western; the Sherlock Holmes books, or any other good mystery; C.S. Forester, or Nordhoff and Hall, or Patrick O'Brien, or any other good sea story; or any science fiction story at all. Fantasy appeals to kids even earlier than the other genres, but much genre literature is like fantasy in this: once you're old enough to read it, it doesn't matter how old you or the characters are. Nine to ninety, as they say.

I suspect this whole talk has been an attempt to justify myself to myself for continuing the young adult trilogy of Earthsea with a trilogy of old adult Earthsea. But I have atoned! My next book, *Gifts*, is a YA with a definitely, absolutely, extremely adolescent hero and heroine. Now, of course, I am thinking of following those two kids to find out what happens to them when they're thirty . . . but that is another story.

Nancy Garden, 2003 Margaret A. Edwards Award

In her 2003 acceptance speech, Margaret A. Edwards winner Nancy Garden discusses some of the intellectual freedom challenges to her novel Annie on My Mind, *and talks about her search as a reader for books with gay characters.*

This is so exciting! I can't believe I'm actually standing here! And I'm very grateful that all of you are sitting out there, especially given SARS and all the many events available to you here at ALA. Thank you for coming.

Last year this award went to one of my heroes, Paul Zindel, who died just three months ago at the young age of 66. I'm sorry to say I never met Paul, but I admired him greatly. *The Pigman* was one of the first YA novels I ever read—if memory serves, I had the privilege of reviewing it for *Junior Scholastic*, for which I worked at the time—and it was one of the books that showed me YA fiction could deal seriously with serious subjects. I was either about to or had just begun to work on my own first novel, which was about a black boy and a white boy who were friends in a racially tense town, and although that book was for somewhat younger kids, *Pigman*, plus Paul's wonderful play *The Effect of*

Gamma Rays on Man-in-the-Moon Marigolds were inspirations to me at the beginning of my career. We have all lost a unique and important voice with his passing, and I am so glad that he won this award before he died.

When I first walked into a library as a small child and went home with an armload of stories, I had no idea that my whole life would be blessed by books. I had no idea that, to paraphrase the Water Rat in *The Wind in the Willows*, one of my greatest pleasures would always be "messing about with books"—reading them, writing them, talking about them, dreaming about them. "Reading rots the mind," we used to joke in my family, quoting a crusty character in Robert Lawson's delightful *Rabbit Hill*. My partner, Sandy, and I repeat that line often when we trip over the piles of books in our house. But rotting, of course, produces rich compost and nourishes growth. Margaret A. Edwards certainly knew that when, in her job at the Enoch Pratt Free Library in Baltimore, she did all she could to encourage reading among teens—the "swarm of beasts," as she affectionately called them, deftly turning a negative term used by 18th-century librarian Jared Bean into a positive one.

I visited the Enoch Pratt Library a couple of years ago to do research, and I remember admiring the extensive and well-planned YA section there. Little did I know or even imagine that one day I would be receiving the award that bears Margaret Edwards's name and honors her for understanding that swarm of beasts, for pioneering in filling their needs at that same library, and for guiding and influencing YA librarians throughout the country.

And little did I know either, way back when I made my first library visit as a child, that years afterward I would be made to feel welcome by other young adult librarians in many parts of the country as I spoke about the First Amendment court case centered on the book you're honoring today, *Annie on My Mind*. That novel, about two teenage girls who fall in love with each other and realize they're gay, was published by Farrar, Straus & Giroux in 1982, and I'm as grateful for the welcome YA librarians have shown to it and to me over the years as I am for this most special and most humbling award.

Annie has a number of older sisters and brothers, books that made her possible. First among them, as some of you have probably heard me say, is Radclyffe Hall's *The Well of Loneliness*, written in England in the 1920s and tried both there and in the U.S. for obscenity because of its subject matter. It was acquitted in the U.S. but banned in its author's native country despite being supported by notables like Virginia Woolf, who apparently didn't much like it, but didn't think it should be suppressed. I devoured Radclyffe Hall's novel when I read it in my teens, having discovered it during my search for books that would help me and Sandy—we had just fallen in love—figure out who we were and how other people dealt with being gay. But except for *The Well of Loneliness*, that was a pretty fruitless search. In the few other books I found—all of which, like *Well*, were for adults—the gay character usually ended up dying in a car crash, committing suicide, being locked away in a mental institution or, if she was a lesbian, being "saved" from homosexuality by a noble Prince Charming who carried her off into the sunset to live happily ever after as a heterosexual. But *The Well of Loneliness*, despite its frequently florid style, its melodrama, and its sad ending, ends on a note of hope. It also ends with a plea for justice and understanding that made me vow to write a book for my people that ended happily.

Years later in 1969, while I was still struggling to write that book, Harper and Row published the late John Donovan's *I'll Get There, It Better Be Worth the Trip*, which broke the longstanding taboo against homosexuality in young adult books. That was followed in the '70s by a few more YAs in which homosexuality was mentioned or even was a central issue. In almost all of those books the gay character is an adult relative or teacher or a teen friend or relative of the straight main character, and in a couple the protagonist is an apparently straight teen who has a brief homosexual affair and/or who recognizes his or her own homosexual feelings without, however, having any real gay consciousness. Although sometimes homosexuality in those early books was still punished by car crashes, suicides, and other disasters, in general it was viewed with gradually increasing sympathy or acceptance.

The strongest of the early books to my way of thinking is Sandra Scoppetone's *Happy Endings Are All Alike*, published in 1974 by Harper and Row. Jaret Tyler, *Happy Endings'* teenage main character, is definitely a lesbian; not only that, she also has a lover. Although Jaret is brutally raped and beaten because of her relationship, and she and her lover part as a result, she emerges undefeated, and at the end of the story, one realizes there is at least hope that someday the two girls may be reunited.

All of these books slowly began to give gay kids assurance that there were other gay people in the world, and that some were even teens like themselves. The books also often provided straight kids increasingly honest insight into what it's like to be gay. And all of them, but especially Donovan's and Scoppetone's, helped give me the courage to go on trying to write a YA novel with a real lesbian protagonist and a definite happy ending.

My first attempt at the book I wanted to write, aside from embarrassingly autobiographical snatches of plays and equally embarrassing melodramatic poetry, was a novel for adults called *For Us Also*, I started writing it in the early or mid-'60s and worked on it for years. Probably the best thing to be said about it is that it taught me a lot about how not to write a novel, and that it led me to coin (or so I thought) the word "soapboxing." In much of *For Us Also* I stood on a figurative authorial soapbox and preached through my main character, Agatha Ronson, known as Ronnie. Through Ronnie I also pleaded with the straight world to understand that we gay folk are really pretty nice people, and shouldn't be treated so unfairly. I groan to admit it, but stylistically, *For Us Also* was a mixture of *The Well of Loneliness* and the Bible, and thank goodness I never tried to have it published. But as I said, it did teach me a lot about how not to write a novel, and showed me I'd better learn more about how *to* write one. I also soon realized that it might be good idea for me to try writing about other subjects before I tackled one that was so dangerously close to my heart, for I had finally learned that, as some of you may know, it is often hardest to write about the things one cares about most.

So for a while I worked on other books, this time for young people, both fiction and nonfiction, that had nothing to do with being gay. I tried to write and sell short stories, too, and, while working for a man who called himself a literary agent but who really ran a sort of editorial agency, I learned how to edit other people's material and even how to ghostwrite novels and plays. (The one that was the most fun was the three-act play whose "author" had provided us with a synopsis consisting of a single sentence for each of its three acts!) I'm pretty sure that it wasn't until I was working as a language arts textbook editor at a real publishing house—Houghton Mifflin—and had managed to get a few of my own books published, that I tried again to write THE book. I called that attempt *Summerhut*, but unfortunately, although I'd stepped partway down off my soapbox by then, I still had one foot on it. I did try to sell *Summerhut*, though, and a very kind editor worked with me on it for a while. But in the end he rejected it, I think wisely.

I dried my tears and after a decent interval, wrote a YA called *Good Moon Rising*. This was a tough one, because instead of having the sense to build my story around just one thing that was important to me—gay characters and issues—I also tried to write about another: theater.

Although my first career goal had been to be a veterinarian, my second had been to work in theater; in fact, I'd had an argument about that with my favorite high school English teacher, who wanted me to be a writer. Even though from the age of eight on, I'd always written and was continuing to do so, I'd actually been "in" theater in my teens and twenties. In fact, for years theater was almost a religion to me; I thought all the world's problems and misunderstandings could probably be solved through the right productions of the right plays. (Would that it were so, but alas, this conviction made me a bit of an artistic snob as well as a hopeless romantic!) I finally left theater, partly because of disillusionment with what was being performed in New York—the artistic snob again—and partly because I was having a hard time getting work. But leaving was so traumatic that for a long time I couldn't even walk into a theater without getting choked up.

Because of all this, writing *Good Moon* was an uncomfortably cathartic experience, and I didn't trust the result. After I finished writing it, I stuffed it into the small red bureau that sits next to my desk and works as a combination file cabinet and table, and I forgot about it until a number of years after *Annie* was published. Then I revised it and Farrar, Straus & Giroux published it. But that's another story.

One rainy noontime not long after I gave up on *Good Moon*, I sat down alone at our kitchen table—Sandy was either at work or at law school. As I began to eat my lunch of tomato soup, the words "It's raining, Annie," popped into my head. Mind you, that's not the usual way an idea for a novel strikes me; it's usually a much longer, much more detailed process. I had no idea who was saying those words or who Annie was, but I knew at once that this was going to be another attempt at THE book. And, thanks to whoever or whatever occasionally gives writers moments like that, it was.

When a long time and many revisions later I thought *Annie* was ready to try to sell, I asked my dear then-agent Dorothy Markinko of McIntosh and Otis to send it to the editor who had so kindly helped me with *Summerhut*; she did, and he decided it wasn't right for him. Dorothy then suggested FSG, who had by then published a book of mine called *Fours Crossing*, a fantasy for kids from 10–14. "Oh, no," I said, horrified and scared. "I don't think they'll want to publish a lesbian novel by an author whose first book for them is a fantasy!"

"Nonsense," Dorothy answered, or words to that effect, and I bless and thank her forever for that. She convinced me, and she sent it off.

And Margaret Ferguson—warm, sensitive, enormously talented, meticulous Margaret Ferguson, who was, I think, an assistant or associate editor at that time—went to bat for it, and wonder of wonders, FSG accepted it! Margaret, who understood what I wanted *Annie* to be as clearly as I did myself, helped me make it a better book than it ever could have been without her. Thank you, Margaret, from the bottom of my heart, both for *Annie* and for working with me so carefully, skillfully, lovingly, and with such uncanny insight on all the many books we've done together since then.

And thank you, FSG, especially for being willing to publish *Good Moon Rising* and my other books about gay kids and issues since *Annie* and for standing by me and by Annie for more than 20 years, through good times and bad, but especially during the two tumultuous years starting in 1993. It was then that *Annie* was burned by a fundamentalist minister in Kansas City and removed from the shelves of school libraries in several school districts in and around Kansas City, in both Kansas and Missouri. As I'm sure some of you know, a group of extraordinarily brave high school students and their equally brave parents in the Olathe, Kansas, district—in which one of the parents taught—brought a First Amendment lawsuit against their school board and superintendent, demanding, as did the district's courageous librarians Jeff Blair and Loretta Wood, that the book be returned to the shelves. The case finally went to Federal District Court in 1995. The hardest part of the trial was listening to the misconceptions about homosexuality voiced by the other side—but there was a bit of comic relief when one of the school board members said she didn't think fiction belonged in a high school library in the first place! Eventually the judge ruled that the book's removal had been unconstitutional. He ordered it put back in Olathe's school libraries.

Thank you, FSG, for letters written and information gathered on *Annie*'s behalf during that battle; especially thank you, Michael Eisenberg, for your support in general both during and after the *Annie* case and for, when I called you from the lawyers' office in Kansas, producing sales figures almost instantly. Thank you, Robbie Mayes, for arranging for me and Sandy to go to Kansas City soon after the book was burned and for warning us and worrying for us when the now-infamous antigay Fred Phelps threatened to picket us (he did, but his bark turned out to be far worse than his bite). Thank you also, Robbie, for your warm friendliness and your skillful editorial input since then. Thank you, sales reps Sean Sullivan and Adrian Krafft for escorting us around town on that first of several trips; thank you, Sean, Adrian—and Sandy, too—for standing ready to be bodyguards in case bodyguards were needed. Luckily, they weren't, but there were some tense moments, and it was a great comfort that you were there.

And thank you, FSG's Jeanne McDermott, for your unfailing tact and humor as you cheerfully and skillfully guided this uncertain author through the "appearances" that later stemmed from the *Annie* lawsuit, and for doing that still.

Others besides the plaintiffs and librarians Jeff and Loretta helped *Annie* survive that ordeal—the other people in Kansas and Missouri who went out of their way to support the book and the First Amendment; the lawyers at Shook, Hardy, and Bacon; the American Civil Liberties Union; PEN American Center; the National Coalition Against Censorship; ALA and YALSA; librarians Linda Waddle, Pat Scales, Ann Carlson Weeks, Dianne McAfee Hopkins, and Alice Stern; thank you, all. Thank you, also, ALA's Office for Intellectual Freedom, especially the indomitable censorship battler and friend to beleaguered authors and librarians, Judith Krug. In time for ALA's annual meeting in, I think, 1994, FSG had a button printed saying SAVE ANNIE in big red letters, and it's thanks to all those people as well that *Annie* was indeed saved and the First Amendment won an important victory.

It's time now, I think, to fast-forward to January 24, 2003, and The Phone Call.

With apologies to Dickens, it was the worst of days, it was the best of days. I woke up that morning full of eager resolve. I had no commitments other than a few Saturday chores; it was going to be a great day on which to work, interruption and crisis-free. HA! Soon after breakfast, when I was about to settle down to draft the final chapter of a new book, our beloved iMac crashed. This was not an average, everyday, annoying-but-easy-to-fix crash. No, this was a megacrash, complete with one of those sinister little smoking bomb icons, which, as those of you who have Macs will know, usually spells Doom with a capital D.

Sandy, who is the computer expert in our household, spent hours trying to repair the damage, while I stood around helplessly bleating things like, "Why don't we look it up again in the manual?" and, "Maybe we should call Apple? Or that nice shop in West Concord that fixed it last time?"

Valiantly, Sandy tried everything she knew and several things she invented. Finally, a while after I had stomped downstairs muttering dark imprecations and trying to tell myself I could always write on an old typewriter or even with a pen during the dark computerless days that obviously were going to stretch far into the future, I heard her cry out in exasperation, "Don't ever let me try to fix this computer again!" I'm afraid I growled something like "I certainly won't!" under my breath—you see the atmosphere that prevailed by then! But—mirabile dictu!—within the next hour Sandy had actually fixed the recalcitrant machine, and I was happily working away on Chapter 17 of a lighthearted 8–12 mystery called, tentatively, *The Case of the Vanishing Valuables*. The day had taken on a much rosier hue.

I had no idea, though, just how rosy it was going to get!

As I approached the end of Chapter 17, the phone rang. I'm not sure, since I was still working, if I answered the phone politely; I hope I did. It was, of course, Rosemary Chance, calling from ALA Midwinter in Philadelphia, only there was so much background noise—I think Rosemary was on a speaker phone—that I had trouble hearing her, and I probably said "Who? What?" stupidly several times. I'd forgotten that this was the Saturday when awards were likely to be announced, and when the words "ALA Midwinter" finally penetrated, I couldn't for the life of me imagine why on earth someone was calling me from there. Poor Rosemary kept being interrupted, too, and was even called away briefly for some reason, so she wasn't able to get to the point of the call right away. In the pauses I racked my brains trying to figure out what that point could be. It can't be an award, I thought; my most recent book hadn't been greeted with the kind of acclaim that presages such things, so what could it possibly be? Maybe someone wanted me to write something? But what? And why, for goodness sake, would ALA want me to do that, and why would they call, especially from Midwinter, to ask? Surely in the unlikely event of such a request, snail mail would suffice, or, in a pinch, e-mail—but of course, the iMac hadn't been working . . .

Finally, through my own fog and the cheerfully excited background noise—all the award committee members, I later learned, were with Rosemary when she called—came the words "Margaret A. Edwards."

Time stopped.

Ohmigosh, I thought. But isn't that . . . ? Oh, God! Could it be . . . ?

And it was. At the point at which Rosemary actually got the words out and I actually understood that *Annie* and I had won the Margaret A. Edwards Award, both Rosemary and I burst into tears, and I have very little memory of anything that followed, except the excited-sounding voices of Eunice Anderson, Sandra A. Farrell, Susan Raboy, and, rising and falling among them, James Edward Cook's happy sparkling laughter. I do remember Rosemary's saying, with great seriousness, something like, "I have to tell you that this award is contingent on your going to Toronto in June to accept it. Will you be able to come?"

I think I replied "You betcha." (And boy am I glad that SARS has allowed us all to do that!) Rosemary of course also told me that I couldn't say anything to anyone till the following Monday—and I of course told Sandy as soon as I got off the phone, and then called our oldest and dearest friends, author-illustrator-editor-teacher Barbara Seuling and her wonderful Renaissance-woman partner, Winnette Glasgow. Barbara immediately went to her computer, looked up the Edwards Award and read me what it said, and soon humility set in as well as joy—for there on that amazing list were many of the writers, along with Paul Zindel, who've been my heroes: especially Walter Dean Meyers, M. E. Kerr, Robert Cormier, Cynthia Voigt, Judy Blume, Chris Crutcher, and others. What a lot to live up to! And when later I found these words: ". . . recognizes an author's work in helping adolescents become aware of themselves and addressing questions about their role and importance in relationships, society, and in the world," I was teary all over again, for that pretty much sums up what I try to do when I write serious fiction.

Thank you, teens both known and unknown who have kept *Annie* alive and who have written so many moving letters sparked by it and my other books; thank you, adult readers of *Annie* as well; thank you, FSG; thank you, friends, colleagues, and supporters: Barbara Seuling, Winnette Glasgow, Linda Zuckerman, Nancy Bond, Betty Levin, Liza Ketchum, Michael Cart, Christine Jenkins, Don Gallo, Cathy Dunn MacRae, Mary K. Chelton, Cynthia Leitich Smith, Michael Thomas Ford, Jim Marks, and my new and most willing agent, Tracey Adams. Thanks also, from long ago, to Tanna, the family matriarch whose favorite people were children and dogs. She taught me to concentrate and, like my parents, fostered my love of books and my imagination; thanks to my parents, who tried to convince me again and again that I could do anything I wanted if I just put my mind to it. I hope all three of them are somehow looking down on this occasion today along with my dear late aunt, Anna Fenn, who always understood the things I tried to do in my serious fiction, and who tried to understand why, especially in my early days, I sometimes wrote about creatures, like vampires, that gave her bad dreams. Thanks as well to oh, so many other people—and especially to my beloved first reader, who has more than once brought me back from the edge of literary disaster and whose literary instincts are so good that several times when I've told Margaret about a new manuscript, Margaret's cautious response has been, "Has Sandy read it yet?" Thank you, Sandy, always and forever.

If there is a single message I've tried to impart to kids in my books it is that it's okay to be different, to discover and fulfill your true identity, to stand up for what you believe, to follow your own dreams—and that kids, as kids, can accomplish wonders. Thank you, YALSA; thank you, SLJ; thank you, Edwards Award Committee for giving me this tremendous gift of encouragement and for thereby spurring me on to continue trying to communicate that message to the "swarm of beasts" I love and admire so much. I promise to try to do my best to live up to this award, to the writers who have won it before me, and to the dedicated librarian for whom it was named.

Judy Blume, 1996 Margaret A. Edwards Award

Blume talks about her desire to create an honest book for teens about sexuality and living with the consequences of their decisions in her 1996 acceptance speech.

FOREVER—A PERSONAL STORY BY JUDY BLUME

I'm as surprised by this honor as many of you. In fact, I was so totally flabbergasted when Marilee reached me in January at my mother-in-law's apartment in Baltimore, I didn't get it at first. I thought she was asking me to serve on a committee to choose a YA author for an award. And what went through my mind was, *funny she should ask me, because I'm not a YA author.*

When it finally sank in that I was being honored and that the book cited was *Forever*, I blurted out, "But *Forever*'s not my best book for that age group!" There was a deadly silence on the other end of the phone. Finally, Marilee asked, "What is?"

"*Tiger Eyes*," I told her.

Another silence. Then, "Oh."

That's when it hit me. You don't argue with someone trying to give you an award. You accept it graciously. And so, Marilee, I am here today to tell you that I am truly honored and grateful—because the next day, on that long train trip to Florida, when I finally digested what you were trying to say, I sat up in my tiny berth, nudged my sleeping husband, and said, "Oh my god! What a gutsy decision they've made—giving me this award in today's fearful climate, with the far right breathing down their necks, demanding family friendly libraries."

As if libraries haven't always been friendly. I can't think of a family friendlier place. I can still see myself at four sitting on the floor of the public library in Elizabeth, New Jersey, sniffing the books and choosing *Madeleine* to take home with me. I loved that book so much I hid it from my mother, so she couldn't return it.

And then the thrill of taking my own small children to the public library—and now, my almost five-year-old grandson, who chooses books for me to read to him. He negotiates at bedtime.

"Seven books, Nonie."

"How about four?"

"How about six."

"We'll see how tired you are."

"I'm never tired."

And so, on that train, I wanted to stand up and cheer, not for myself, but because this committee is sending those would-be censors a powerful message—a message that you are out there protecting our young people's right to read and to choose books freely; a message that you recognize and respect my need and every writer's need to create in an atmosphere free from fear; a message that no one individual or group is going to frighten you or intimidate you—and if that's not what you're saying, don't tell me, okay?

As Carolyn Caywood wrote in *SLJ* [*School Library Journal*], she'd rather have heard what went on in that committee meeting than what I have to say today. I think we all would, Carolyn.

When I began to write in the late sixties and publish in the early seventies, I had never heard of a category called YA books, which is probably why I've never thought of myself as a YA writer. So I did some research in preparation for this talk. It was Dorothy Broderick who put me in touch with Betty Carter, who told me YA has a revisionist history. There are those who will argue that *Little Women* was the first YA novel, an idea that really appeals to me.

Betty also told me a wonderful *Forever* story about her daughter and her first summer at sleepaway camp following fifth grade. And how, when Betty asked what was the best thing about camp, her daughter said, "I read *Forever*, Mom! Each of us chipped in twenty-five cents to buy it but then we made the boys pay fifty cents apiece if they wanted to read it." For this, Betty spent a hefty amount to give her young daughter a summer experience she'd never forget. There are a lot of *Forever* stories.

Until I wrote *Forever* in 1975, I had never written about older teenagers. My characters were the tens, elevens, and twelves, the kids on the brink—full of secret thoughts and active imaginations. Sometimes they had older siblings, but I wasn't interested in their points of view. Maybe because my own teenage years were a fifties mix of the bland and the boring, when every feeling and concern was kept tightly under wraps, when we all pretended to be so happy, so fine. *What . . . problems? Not us!*

Then, in '75, Randy, my 14-year-old daughter, a voracious reader, was racing through a group of books a librarian friend of mine referred to as "the pregnant book"—you know the ones—if a girl succumbs, if she gives in, she faces pregnancy, abandonment, a gruesome illegal abortion, even death or, at best, a long train trip to another place. Sexuality linked with punishment.

In those books, girls never do it because they want to. They're passive, not active participants. They're never sexually turned on. And in those books, boys have no feelings, boys never have their hearts broken. So when Randy asked, "Couldn't there be a book where two nice kids from nice families do it and no one has to die?" I began to think about sexuality linked with responsibility. About young people making decisions and living with the consequences of those decisions.

Now, I've always believed that the best books come from some place deep inside and that a good writer doesn't write to order, doesn't write what somebody else needs to read, although sometimes it turns out to be what somebody else needs to read. And maybe the reason I told Marilee *Forever* isn't my best book is because of the way it was conceived. I'm reconsidering now, Marilee. Maybe it doesn't matter where the idea originates, maybe the only thing that matters is how deeply it's felt.

Walter Dean Myers, 1994 Margaret A. Edwards Award

Accepting the 1994 Margaret A. Edwards Award, Walter Dean Myers talks in his speech about his goals as a writer, among them to amuse, entertain, divert, and stimulate young readers and also to recognize and celebrate the humanity of every young person.

I have spent a good part of my life in self-examination, wondering where I fit into the great schemes of life, and if life did, indeed, have great schemes. On a personal level I wondered if I were as bright as the next person, as talented, or basically good. I wondered what to think of myself and what others thought of me. The consciousness of self, this attempt to realize the world through an understanding of one's own psyche, is core element of the writer. We examine ourselves in minute detail and then draw conclusions, colored by the biases of our own experience, about the rest of the world. Somewhere along the way we establish as insight the discovery of our own humanity, those weaknesses and strengths that capacity to love and hate, that ability to strive and fail and to strive yet again, that brings humility to our work. But it is only when we acquire the ability to look beyond ourselves and to recognize the humanity of others that we become truly interesting. It is the extension of humanity to our character that makes them recognizable to our readers, that brings the shadow of familiarity to our plots.

But there is more. Once we release our characters from our own needs, once we allow them to exist freely within the worlds we have discovered for them, we begin to create ideals. In these ideals we suggest how we want the world to be, and how we should relate to each other. We become so bold that we even dare to say what humankind is and what it should become. The drive to create these ideals, the urge to be this bold and this daring, both informs and drives my writing. By extension, I believe that this confluence of author, reader, and ideal is at the heart of our best literature for young adults, and should be.

The United States was created as an amazingly wealthy state, and has continued to be so, but it is also a state in which many of its children have fared poorly. I am reminded of all those children enslaved on plantations prior to the Civil War. I am reminded of the white children that Lewis Hines photographed in the mines. I think of the Jewish, Irish, and Italian children in the New York slums at the turn of the century. I think of the children of migrant workers, of Appalachian children working in the apple orchards in West Virginia. I think of Japanese children interned in camps during the Second World War. I think of Indian children living in poverty on reservations. What these children had in common, beside their grinding poverty, was that they were put away from the public view. Not merely overlooked, but put away. It took the likes of a Lewis Hines, a Jacob Riis, or a Dorothea Lange to bring these children to the attention of the world, to rescue them from being nonpersons. It seems that, even in our wealthy country, there are always children that need to be rescued from some obscure hell, to be brought into the light of recognition so that we can no longer avoid looking at their suffering.

Today we are hiding away our children again. We are replacing their likenesses with images of monsters. We are telling ourselves that we fear our children, and that we need to deal with them more harshly. Forgetting that our children are who we are, that their souls reflect the love we have given, or not given; that their hates and prejudices reflect what we have taught them, we pretend not to know who they are. As we turn away from our children, our young adults in particular, as we lock our doors, as we clutch our wallets closer and lower the age when we can incarcerate them, they cease to know us. And we stop knowing them. What's more, we all, children and adults, move further and further away from a sense of the ideal.

I don't believe that I can fly, walk on water, or stop wars in foreign countries. But I can write and I do publish and I believe, that for whatever difference it makes, I will let down my bucket where I am. What I can do is help make all our children and all our young adults visible again. I can help begin the process of peeling away labels they have been burdened with, that diminish their humanity. What's more, I can help to create in story form a common ground of understanding, the arena of ideals.

The special place of the young adult novel should be in its ability to address the needs of the reader to understand his or her relationships with the world, with each other, and with adults. The young adult novel often allows the reader to directly identify with a protagonist of similar interests and development. In the process the novel can also amuse, entertain, divert, and stimulate the reader to enjoy the process of this communication. But most important it allows the reader to be included in the society of the book. For many young people the only place in the world they find themselves included is in the pages of novels.

My own life as an adolescent was filled with trouble and inner turmoil. A good and avid reader, the books and ideas with which I tried to cope were a forever distance from where I needed to know was how unique were my thoughts, my feelings as a black teenager in Harlem. I needed to know if it was really okay to worry about the existence of God, and if it was all right being black in a country that sometimes lynched black people. Was it normal for me to feel apart from my parents? Did it have anything to do with the differences between my life and theirs? Was my penchant for staying home and reading far into the night a good thing, or was I somehow peculiar? Were there other boys my age who secretly wrote poems and hid them? Was it true, as it seemed to be, that my value had to be reinterpreted in terms of some European concept? Was it all right to be me, more comfortable with books than with people, more at ease talking about basketball than Mozart, more interested in seeing the black women shopping in the market under the elevated tracks than in going to the museums?

And what of the young adults I considered my friends? Were they all right too? Their parents were janitors and factory workers. Their brothers fought in the trenches and died in the streets. How did they fit into life's grand scheme? If there was an ideal, did it mean that my friends had to be rejected? It was clear that they were not being described as part of the ideal I found in my recommended reading lists. I loved Mark Twain, but Twain didn't talk about the streets I knew, or about my church, or my father stealing pound cake from the supermarket so that we wouldn't have to go to bed hungry. Mark Twain didn't, nor did Thomas Mann or Jack London, talk about my mother working in a factory and coming home with her ankles so swollen she could hardly stand. How did my parents, my family, and friends relate to the world in which I found myself?

When I began to publish I found myself drawn to these questions, many of which I have never adequately answered. I keep trying. I feel myself drawn to them more than ever today. These seem to be so many young people who are being "shut away" from American society, who don't have even a hint of how they fit into their communities, or even their own families. I see young people who are bewildered in their search for roles within the larger society. Sometimes they are painfully aware that they are not wanted in the larger society. Sometimes we are painfully aware that we don't want them even as we despair at their behavior. Even as we look to protect ourselves from them.

These young people need to talk to other young people like themselves, and when they can't find the other people to talk to, or when, as is often the case, they are too inarticulate to do so, then they need to read about other young people. When I say that they are inarticulate I don't mean that they have no words. They have words such as pain, and frustration, and anger. But their articulation is limited by the language of values from which they are excluded. It is this language of values which I hope to bring to my books. I would be the voice of those young adults who come from the same shadows of past that I knew, even as my fellow young adult writers give voice to the children of their own pasts. I want to bring values to those who have not been valued, and I want to etch those values in terms of the ideal.

Young people need ideals which identify them, and their lives, as central to the ideals. They need guideposts which tell them what they can be, should be, and indeed, are. Paul Tillich, in *The Dynamics of Faith*, speaks of "the ultimate dimension in which man lives." This dimension has little to do with an innate state of humankind. It is, indeed, what we learn to be, the dimension we learn to assume. If we do not expose children and young adults to these "ultimate dimensions," if by silent assent we agree that they are not capable of a greater human dimension, then we are contributing to their destruction. If we do not write about all of our children, write about them with hard truths and a harder compassion, then we have, in a very significant way, failed our own futures.

So what I am saying, again, is that I want to amuse my readers, to entertain them, to divert them, and stimulate them. But I also want to talk to them about ideals, about not only what human experience can be but what their particular human experience can be. I want to recognize the humanity of every young person and find ways to celebrate that humanity and to offer the young person the means to celebrate whatever self is found in the mirror. These are my offerings to young adults, and to myself.

I am fortunate to be able to do what I want to with my life, to write, to tell my stories. I am fortunate to have the opportunity to write for young adults and to be part of this vital community of writers and book people.

Finally, I am deeply honored that my work has received the recognition of the Margaret A. Edwards Committee and to be able to stand alongside the distinguished group of past honorees.

Thank you.

Richard Peck, 1990 Margaret A. Edwards Award

Placing himself in the lineage of Mark Twain and Booth Tarkington, Richard Peck talks about the function of fiction in his acceptance speech for the 1990 Margaret A. Edwards Lifetime Achievement Award.

LOVE IS NOT ENOUGH

As you will have noticed all by yourselves, life is a bad novel. I'd learned that I'd be coming to Chicago for the Annual Conference of the American Library Association this year when I was in the third lock of the Panama Canal. The ship was a great white ocean liner embarked from South America on the day Noriega surrendered, and bound for Costa Rica.

On a hot January day I was having lunch on the Lido Deck with the Canal Zone moving slowly past, a landscape of bougainvillea and gun barrels, when I was paged to the radio room. It was a wavery call from Roger Sutton in Chicago, and behind him a committee chorus. I heard news from another world, as welcome as it was surprising.

You may well ask what business I had in the third lock of the Panama Canal. Or for that matter why I was spending the winter adrift among tropical ports. It would more benefit the stations in the life of Stephen King or Danielle Steel, though not, of course, in the same accommodations.

But I was working my passage. I am the ship's lecturer. I'd already delivered an address called, "Blood-soaked Panama, from Balboa to Noriega," and history was fast overtaking my speech notes. You mightn't think ships need lecturers, but they seem to. As a result in this entire room, I'm the only member of the Greek Seamen's Union. Writers are, after all, at sea most of the time one way or another anyway. Besides, I once found a novel on board that ship. Its title is *Those Summer Girls I Never Met*, and it's about grandmother power.

On a ship, the peer group isn't a pack of teenagers in status sneakers flashing drug gold and gang signs; it's a flying wedge of grandparents, with their own clothes and music, their own language and symbolism. These members of the AARP are strangely like the inmates of a high school. They move in a group and demand to be recognized as individuals. They're restless all morning, waiting for lunch. You have to tell them everything three times, and then they swear they never heard it (though in their case it's often true).

But I got a novel from them, in which two teenagers who didn't even want to go on the cruise find that it's a voyage of discovery as they come to know their grandparents as human beings. That seemed a theme worth exploring for a generation of the young who no longer even have to write thank-you notes for gifts from grandparents, and so they rob themselves of their own roots.

Books and voyages are both little lifetimes, with beginnings, middles, and ends. They even call the place where the voyage begins "a berth." And voyages and books are both communities. A ship in fact is nothing but a small town with everybody's nose in everybody else's business. When I received my first-ever radio telephone call, I found out just how small a ship is. I might point out that this was the Christmas holiday cruise, and so quite a few librarians were aboard, librarians who had married wisely and well. It wasn't an hour after the phone call before I was accosted I an elevator by a California librarian. "I've just heard your news," she said. "You've won the Newberry."

I did what anyone would do under the circumstance. I gazed at the floor and said, "Well, it was a long time coming."

"You can say that again," the California librarian replied. "I thought you should have had it for *A Day No Pigs Would Die*."

And so I thank you for this award. No good deed goes unpunished, and I have been. And I've learned nothing. Before the summer is over, I'll have run away to sea again. A novel is a community, more tightly knit than the community where the reader lives, and fortunately I came from one. It was a town called Decatur, Illinois, and I can't prove that I could have been a writer from any other place. It was a town at the exact midpoint between Mark Twain's Hannibal and the Indianapolis of Booth Tarkington. It was Mark Twain who invented boyhood, and Booth Tarkington discovered adolescence because he wrote a novel called *Alice Adams* about a girl who went to a party when it would have been so much safer to stay at home.

I came from a whole community. It wasn't a suburb, and so even a child could see money earned well as well as money spent. It wasn't inner city, and so the government didn't give checks to children for having children. It was a town in a time when teenagers were considered guilty until proven innocent, which is fair enough.

Decatur was that place on the map where the puritan ethic had gone to die. There we worked "for the night is coming," which isn't a bad plan for a writer. Every time you set foot outdoors in Decatur, your reputation was on the line. That makes a writer too, because a novel is gossip to pass as art.

It was in that small town that my mother read to me before I could read for myself. She gave me what is now called "pre-reading experience," except I actually got it. I doubt if she was trying to make of me a published writer. She was trying to get me ready for first grade. And so she sent me off to elementary school with a vocabulary I can't find in the letters high school students send me now. She read *Alice in Wonderland* to me. I might not have remembered that, except my aunt came into the room that afternoon and said, "What are you reading to him?"

And my mother said, "I wish I knew."

That made a reader out of me right there. I thought my mother knew everything, but in books there were even greater depths to plumb. I was a convert. And lucky for me because nobody but a reader ever became a writer.

I grew up, a reader, in town where the library was a house of books. It wasn't a high-tech, low-impact information-retrieval gridlock system. On those library shelves was Mark Twain, there when I needed to know that a novel could speak in the voices I heard around me in my town, that a novel could look at the world through the eyes of the young.

From Mark Twain we learn the Sacred Secret, to write in love and anger. Love for the world and anger at the world made wrong, at the callowness of the young before us and of the young we were. Anger at the recalcitrance of the English language whose words don't drop from heaven to pattern the page as nonwriters think they do.

Loving the young is not enough, as we see from the bitter experiences of their parents. Never hold the young responsible for the consequences of their actions because they are only the victims of capitalist society or welfare state or (more cautiously) victims of one another will not make a writer.

We have an ugly American habit of forgiving those we cannot control. When we learn that the young are more racially bigoted than their own parents; when we learn that the young don't believe they can become pregnant or drug-addicted unless they want to—the parent goes looking for scapegoats, but the writer is moved to write.

I wrote a novel in love and anger, and I found it not far from here, though I might have found it anywhere. I came across it at New Trier High School in Winnetka, some years after that very school declined to hire me as an English teacher. There at the end of the opulent parking lot was a novel. It's about the adolescent peer group now that they have the authority that once rested with teachers and parents. It's about the greatest quest of adolescence, the search for a power source, to give your life a shape, to do your thinking for you. It's the story of a girl who believes her mother is never right and that the girl who commands her peer group at school is never wrong. A tragedy, of course, called *Princess Ashley*. It's a novel on the theme I most believe in—my recurring theme. Since no reviewer has ever discovered what that theme is, I will tell you: *that you will never begin to grow up until you declare your independence from your peers.* All novels of serious intent incite to rebellion, and this is mine.

It came of being a teacher, and I was a teacher as long as I could be. There at the front of the room I noticed that nobody ever grows up in a group. People grow up one at a time if at all, like a girl named Blossom Culp. It was as a teacher that I grew skeptical of people in groups, whether in the classroom or the faculty meeting. That works for a writer because a novel is a celebration of the individual.

Offering books as gifts to the literature minority of the young as writers, as librarians, is a high calling, but it's uphill work, and they are deaf to most of our entreaties. We tremble for our mortality and savor every day; they drive drunk because they cannot die. We believe practice make perfect; they've been getting grades on rough drafts. We believe you ought to make long plans and aim high; most of them would prefer a car to a high-school education and have proved it. We want to live in the widest worlds possible; they've been told by their own schools that foreign language is an elective!

Lucky for them we writers and librarians came along. Lucky for them there exists a field of books optimistically called "Young Adult," to point out that the function of fiction is to prepare for life, not to avoid it. Lucky for me to be here to thank you for the award you've conferred on my books. Writers love irony and have been known to overwork it. And here is another irony: an award from librarians comes from the very people who should be receiving an award because librarians are the official representatives of writers, living and dead. Librarians are a writer's best hope for reaching a generation of readers who do not read reviews and who go to schools where they cannot win letter sweaters for literacy. I wish the world beyond these walls knew that we librarians and writers are colleagues with our hopes in tandem and our fates entwined, and with our backs to the same wall while the American school system persists in handing out high-school diplomas to graduates who cannot read them.

Nor can our publishers save us, though my publisher, George Nicholson, gave me my start. He accepted the first line of fiction I ever wrote, and he's accepted every young adult book since. But for him, I wouldn't be with you now. But for George Nicholson, I'd still have tenure somewhere. But the next best thing to tenure is a good agent, and so I'm grateful to Sheldon Fogelman.

We are united in this room as publishers and agents, librarians and parents and writers, by the same motive: to put the right books in the right hands and then hope for the best—books that depend on the goodwill and the hard work of librarians, who may just be the only adults on call in many young lives.

Writers write in all the voices we can find, except our own. We strain to hear young voices inaudible to their own parents, voices they fear to raise within the hearing of their powerful peers. And so I conclude in the voice of a young reader:

> I read: because one life isn't enough,
>   And in the pages of a book I can be anybody.
>
> I read: because the words that build the story become mine,
>   To build my life.
>
> I read: not for happy endings but for new beginnings;
>   I'm just beginning myself, and I wouldn't mind a map.
>
> I read: because I have friends who don't, and young though they are,
>   They're beginning to run out of material.
>
> I read: because every journey begins at the library,
>   And it's time for me to start packing.
>
> I read: because one of these days I'm going to get out of this town,
>   and I'm going to go everywhere and meet everybody, and I want to be
>   ready.

Chapter 5

The Printz Award

Introductory Overview

Michael Cart

The Michael L. Printz Award is presented annually by the Young Adult Library Services Association to the author of the best young adult book of the year, "best" being defined solely in terms of literary merit. Because the first Printz Award was presented in the year 2000 (to Walter Dean Myers for his novel *Monster*), it was widely hailed—at its creation—as being "a new award for a new millennium."

Though it was, inarguably, a new award, the need for a young adult book prize that would be analogous to the Newbery Medal for children's literature had been discussed for years, though no action to transform discussion into reality had ever been undertaken. This was due to a variety of factors: Young adult literature, having emerged only in the late 1960s, was regarded by many as a genre in its infancy that was nothing more than a subgenre of children's literature; the "parent" literature, on the other hand, was already several centuries old as a literary form when the Newbery Medal was created in the early 1920s (the first medal was awarded in 1922 to Hendrik Willem van Loon for *The Story of Mankind*). Also, after a strong start in the 1970s, young adult literature had gone into a period of first relative and then precipitous decline in the 1980s and early 1990s; perhaps accordingly, the genre had—like the late comedian Rodney Danger-field—never gotten any respect, being dismissed by academics and critics as little more than formulaic problem novels and genre fiction. In fact, the very term "young adult literature" was widely regarded as an oxymoron. Last—and perhaps most important—the corporate culture of ALA was regarded, frankly, as being so Byzantine that the creation of a young adult book prize might well be, at worst, impossible, or, at best, roughly equivalent to one of the labors of Hercules.

This all began to change in 1994, the catalyst being a YALSA preconference held in Miami. Though the ostensible agenda for this occasion was the quinquennial selection of the 100 best books for young adults (in this case those published between 1967 and 1992), the planning committee, chaired by Pam Spencer (later Pam Spencer Holley), and consisting of Mike Printz, Barb Lynn, Judy Druse, and myself recognized it as an opportunity to call the attention of the library and publishing community to the parlous state of the genre's health and to underscore the imperative importance of the field's revival.

Two authors have been awarded both a Printz award and an Honor award:

David Almond for *Kit's Wilderness* (Printz Winner 2001) and *Skellig* (Printz Honor 2000)
John Green for *Looking for Alaska* (Printz Winner 2006) and *An Abundance of Katherines* (Printz Honor 2007)

It would be an oversimplification to argue that the result was an overnight renaissance of young adult literature. But the passionate discussion the event generated, along with a spate of articles in the professional literature, did succeed in reviving national interest in the field. Of equal importance was the sudden spike in the teenage population that began in 1993 (following a fifteen-year decline from 1977 to 1992). This newly expansive market, coupled with the avid encouragement of the library profession, resulted in a revival of publisher interest. To further expand the potential readership, publishers began encouraging authors to write edgier, more sophisticated and even experimental fiction. As a result, a new literary form quickly began to emerge and, by the late 1990s, people were talking excitedly about a "new golden age of young adult literature." Improbably, the form had found a new aesthetic.

This new aesthetic then met with opportunity in the spring of 1998 when, as president of YALSA and with the encouragement of Deputy Executive Director Linda Waddle, I appointed a nine-member task force to investigate the feasibility of establishing the long-overdue young adult book award. Exercising my presidential prerogative, I appointed myself as chair. Reaching for professional diversity, I appointed, as committee members, two editors, Marc Aronson and David Gale, both of whom had spoken at the 1994 preconference; a reviewer and critic, Hazel Rochman of *Booklist* magazine; a reading specialist, Dr. Gwendolyn Davis; two public librarians, Kirsten Edwards and Ed Sullivan; and two school librarians, Frances Bradburn and Mary Purucker.

Markus Zusak has won two Printz Honors: *I Am the Messenger* (2006) and *The Book Thief* (2007).

The task force first met at the 1998 Annual Conference, held that year in Washington, DC. Our mission was "to investigate the feasibility of an annual award for the best young adult book based solely on literary merit, to establish criteria for selection with necessary policies and procedures, and to explore the mechanisms for effectuating the award." The task force was unanimous in its belief that an award was long overdue and that its creation, along with the stipulation that it be awarded solely on the basis of literary merit or excellence, was essential to serve notice on the world that young adult literature had arrived . . . *as literature*. It was also quickly agreed that the award would be given to the author of a young adult book, not a book for young adults; in other words, a book published as an adult title, though having interest to young adult readers, would not be eligible. This, again, was a conscious decision made to underscore the importance to readers of a separate, distinct body of literature written and published for young adults, whom the task force defined as "readers twelve to eighteen years of age" (YALSA's official definition).

As for criteria, the task force was anxious that these should reflect the newly expansive nature of young adult literature. Thus, it was stipulated that the award was not limited to works of fiction but could also be given to nonfiction, poetry, short story collections, anthologies, works of sequential art (i.e., graphic novels), works of joint authorship, and—reflecting the international explosion of interest in young adult literature—works first published in other countries (and other languages).

The third part of the mission—"to explore the mechanisms for effectuating the award"—which had seemed, at first, to be the most forbidding turned out, on investigation, to be the simplest: the task force's recommendation that the award be established required only the approval of the YALSA Board of Directors and the ALA Awards Committee (since this would be a divisional award, ALA Council approval was not required).

> Walter Dean Myers, who was honored with an Edwards Award in 1994, won the first Printz Award in 2000 for *Monster*.

The task force's desire to seize the symbolic opportunity of launching this award in the year 2000 ("a new award for a new millennium") meant putting its work on a very fast track, however. It was necessary to draft a preliminary report for approval by the YALSA Executive Committee before the end of 1998 so that the final report could be presented to both the full YALSA Board and the ALA Awards Committee at the 1999 Midwinter meeting. This meant doing a considerable body of work online between Annual and Midwinter (for details, see Cart, 1998, 1999). Discussion focused on three chief areas: one was the establishment of a more expansive definition of the term "literary merit." To accomplish that I appointed a subcommittee consisting of Hazel Rochman, David Gale, and Mary Purucker. Their recommendations were adopted as presented and are now incorporated into the Printz Award Policies and Procedures (www.ala.org/yalsa/printz).

A second area of discussion involved the timing of the award; initially consideration was given to following the model of the National Book Awards and announcing a short list of nominated titles either during the October observation of Teen Read Week or at the Youth Media Awards Press Conference; the winner would then be announced during National Library Week. This idea was, however, quickly abandoned, and it was decided that the award announcement and presentation should follow the model of the other ALA youth awards. This decision then fostered considerable discussion as to precisely when, during the Annual Conference, the award (and honor awards) should be presented. In the early years they were incorporated into the annual Margaret A. Edwards Award Luncheon, though this was never regarded as satisfactory and was soon replaced by an increasingly gala ceremony held on the Monday evening of the Annual Conference.

Even before the first meeting of the task force *Booklist* had offered to cosponsor the award, and this offer was gladly accepted. As a result, a *Booklist* consultant serves as a nonvoting but otherwise fully participating member of the nine-person Printz Committee. It was also decided, early in the process, that four members and the chair should be appointed by the vice president/president elect of YALSA and the remaining four members should be elected by the YALSA membership. (Because of timing considerations, however, the entire first committee was appointed by then–Vice President/President Elect Jana Fine.) The task force patterned the mechanics of actually selecting a winner after those governing the Newbery Medal, including procedures for weighted voting. This led to an amusing mathematical anomaly, though it was not discovered until the 2005 Printz committee began its deliberations and realized that the weighted balloting was based on the Newbery Committee's having fifteen members, while the Printz committee has only nine. The discrepancy was quickly corrected, though not without causing some initial consternation.

The Printz Award honors books in diverse formats!

Look for:

Screenplay: Walter Dean Myers, *Monster* (Printz Winner 2000)

Poetry: Virginia Euwer Wolff, *True Believer* (Printz Honor 2002), Jan Greenberg Abrams, *Heart to Heart: New Poems Inspired by Twentieth-Century American Art* (Printz Honor 2002), and Helen Frost, *Keesha's House* (Printz Honor 2004)

Graphic novel: Gene Luen Yang, *American Born Chinese* (Printz Winner 2007)

Short stories: Margo Lanagan, *Black Juice* (Printz Honor 2006)

Diary: Louise Rennison, *Angus, Thongs, and Full Frontal Snogging: Confessions of Georgia Nicolson* (Printz Honor 2001)

Nonfiction: Jack Gantos, *Hole in My Life* (Printz Honor 2003), Marilyn Nelson, *A Wreath for Emmett Till* (Printz Honor 2006), and Elizabeth Partridge, *John Lennon: All I Want Is the Truth, a Photographic Biography* (Printz Honor 2006)

Transparency and membership participation were very important to the task force throughout the course of its work. As a result, its preliminary report was published on both the YALSA-L and YALSA-BK electronic discussion lists a month prior to the Midwinter meeting. This report was then presented to the YALSA Board on Friday morning of Midwinter, when it was approved in concept. It was then presented for discussion at a member forum that evening. Saturday morning, it was taken before the ALA Awards Committee, which approved it unanimously. The YALSA Board then adopted the report, which had been slightly revised based on member input received from the listserv postings and the member forum. Specifically, these changes involved abandoning the idea of a short list and establishing a more conventional awards calendar; that is, the award committee would meet twice, at Annual and Midwinter. The winner and honor titles (if any) would be announced at the Midwinter Youth Media Awards press conference and the winners would receive their awards at the following Annual Conference. It was also agreed that, instead of the committee members serving staggered three-year terms, as had been initially proposed, they should simply serve one-year terms. The task force had also struggled to find a method for involving the membership in naming the award, but the YALSA Board, following a brief discussion, chose, simply, to name it in honor of the late Michael L. Printz (in fact, this possibility had earlier been discussed by the task force).

Following the formal acceptance of the task force recommendations, the YALSA Board charged the task force with the further responsibility of creating operating procedures for the committee. These were finished and adopted by the YALSA Executive Committee in March of 1999 and were immediately conveyed to the first Printz committee, which had been appointed shortly after the Midwinter meeting.

Printz is the award for first-time novelists!

If you want to read an author at the beginning of his or her career, look to the Printz list. Many first novels have been given the Printz or a Printz honor. Among them are:

Terry Trueman, *Stuck in Neutral* (Printz Honor 2001)
An Na, *A Step from Heaven* (Printz Winner 2002)
Helen Frost, *Keesha's House* (Printz Honor 2004)
Meg Rosoff, *How I Live Now* (Printz Winner 2005)
John Green, *Looking for Alaska* (Printz Winner 2006)

In the years since, a total of 10 Printz winners have been selected, along with 33 honor titles. Together they represent the splendid diversity that is contemporary young adult literature, and they serve as well to define, by example, the true meaning of the term "literary excellence." The award has been influential in encouraging publishers to enrich the field with a growing body of literary, character-driven fiction, and creative nonfiction. Meanwhile authors from England and Australia have been honored, along with American writers, while such diverse forms as short story collections, anthologies, nonfiction, and graphic fiction have also been recognized.

The Printz Award has done what awards should ideally do: recognize achievement, call attention to a body of literature, and encourage writers and publishers to take creative risks and pursue excellence and, thereby, elevate the quality and stature of the literature. As a result, the lives of countless young readers have been enriched and, perhaps, even transformed. In these important ways, the Printz Award has already proven to be not only a new award for a new millennium but also an award of enduring importance for all times and all seasons.

References

Cart, Michael. 1998. "Begetting an Award." *Booklist*, September: 108–109.

Cart, Michael. 1999. "Creating the Michael L. Printz Award." *Journal of Youth Services in Libraries* (Summer): 30–34. Available: www.ala.org/yalsa/booklistsawards/printzaward/aboutprintz/michaellprintz.htm.

The Printz Winners: An Annotated Bibliography

Pam Spencer Holley

2008 Prizes

PRINTZ WINNER

MCCAUGHREAN, GERALDINE. *The White Darkness*. HarperTempest.
> Battling an inscrutable villain in the frozen South Pole, Symone learns survival skills from her imaginary companion, the long-dead explorer Titus Oates.

Subjects: Deception, Survival, Antarctica

PRINTZ HONOR BOOKS

CLARKE, JUDITH. *One Whole and Perfect Day*. Front Street.
> Lily, the sensible one in her quirky Australian family, longs to fit in with her classmates even while belittling their shallow interests. Then Grandpa goes berserk and Lily falls in love.

Subjects: Grandparents, Brothers and Sisters, Family Problems, Australia

HEMPHILL, STEPHANIE. *Your Own, Sylvia: A Verse Portrait of Sylvia Plath*. Alfred A. Knopf. **NF**
> Hemphill's powerful portrait uses verse to shed light on the life of the gifted poet, who most people know for her tragic end.

Subjects: Sylvia Plath

JENKINS, A. M. *Repossessed.* HarperTeen.
> A bored demon takes over the body of a sullen teen to find out how humans live, changing the lives of those around him.

Subjects: Spirit Possession, Conduct of Life, Interpersonal Relations, High Schools, Devil

KNOX, ELIZABETH. *Dreamquake: Book Two of the Dreamhunter Duet.* Frances Foster Books.
> In the second volume of the *Dreamhunter Duet,* Laura searches for master dreams to reverse the effects of a government conspiracy, only to discover an even more sinister plot.

Subjects: Dreams, Family Life, Fantasy

2007 Prizes

PRINTZ WINNER

YANG, GENE LUEN. *American Born Chinese.* First Second.
> A Chinese folk hero and two Asian-American students are linked in a graphic representation of cultural stereotypes, racism, and self-acceptance.

Subjects: Graphic Novel, Chinese Americans, Family, Mythology

PRINTZ HONOR BOOKS

ANDERSON, M.T. *The Astonishing Life of Octavian Nothing, Traitor to the Nation,* Volume 1: *The Pox Party.* Candlewick.
> Regarded as a slave, but studied by scientists while receiving a classical education, Octavian ponders the irony of his country fighting for a freedom he will never have.

Subjects: African Americans, Racism, Science Experiments, Historical Novel

GREEN, JOHN. *An Abundance of Katherines.* Dutton.
> After being dumped by the 19th Katherine, a road trip introduces Colin to a non-Katherine, and together they develop a theorem for predicting the length of relationships.

Subjects: Dating, Mathematics

HARTNETT, SONYA. *Surrender.* Candlewick.
> A curious friendship develops between "good Anwell" and "destructive Finnegan" who share a love for their thieving dog Surrender.

Subjects: Thriller, Dogs, Grief, Guilt, Arson

ZUSAK, MARKUS. *The Book Thief.* Knopf.
> With stolen books to sustain her even before she can read, Liesel survives World War II in Germany, though her life is too often touched by death.

Subjects: Germany, Holocaust, World War II, Books, Death

2006 Prizes

PRINTZ WINNER

GREEN, JOHN. *Looking for Alaska*. Dutton.
"Pudge" Halter discovers a new life when he arrives at an Alabama boarding school and tastes freedom, guilty pleasures, and an amazing girl named Alaska.
Subjects: High School, Friendship, Death

PRINTZ HONOR BOOKS

LANAGAN, MARGO. *Black Juice*. Eos.
Ten short stories offer readers entry into worlds familiar yet strange and surprising, from clown-killing assassins to rescue elephants or a tardy bride.
Subjects: Fantasy, Short Stories

NELSON, MARILYN. *A Wreath for Emmett Till*. Houghton Mifflin. **NF**
Fifteen intricately connected poems tell of the lynching of Emmett Till for whistling at a white woman.
Subjects: Till, Emmet; African Americans; Lynching; Hate Crimes; Mississippi; Murder

PARTRIDGE, ELIZABETH. *John Lennon: All I Want Is the Truth, a Photographic Biography*. Viking. **NF**
Lennon's words, photos, and music show the creativity, anger, and confusion behind the public face of this talented musician.
Subjects: Musicians; Creativity; Lennon, John

ZUSAK, MARKUS. *I Am the Messenger*. Knopf.
After incompetent cabbie Ed accidentally halts a robbery, he receives playing cards with anonymous messages to help, or hurt, specific people.
Subjects: Taxicab Drivers, Heroes, Self Esteem

2005 Prizes

PRINTZ WINNER

ROSOFF, MEG. *How I Live Now*. Wendy Lamb Books/Random House.
Visiting her cousins in England in the midst of an unexpected occupation by terrorist forces, Daisy manages to find true love and a sense of family.
Subjects: Dystopia, Family, England

PRINTZ HONOR BOOKS

OPPEL, KENNETH. *Airborn*. HarperCollins.
Cabin boy aboard an airship, Matt retrieves a battered solo airship, which leads to a pirate attack, stranding on an island, and discovery of "cloud cats."
Subjects: Fantasy, Airships

SCHMIDT, GARY D. *Lizzie Bright and the Buckminster Boy*. Clarion.
  Based on a true event, the new minister's son befriends Lizzie, who lives on an island populated by former slaves, until the town decides it needs the island for development.
Subjects: Maine, Progress, Racism, Friendship, Historical Fiction

STRATTON, ALLAN. *Chanda's Secrets*. Annick Press.
  In southern Africa the danger of AIDS encircles Chanda and her family; when she is left to care for her siblings, she ensures that each is tested for the disease.
Subjects: AIDS, Death, Family

2004 Prizes

PRINTZ WINNER

JOHNSON, ANGELA. *The First Part Last*. Simon & Schuster Books for Young Readers.
  Told in alternating chapters, Bobby and his girlfriend Nia reveal the love they shared then, as well as the growing affection Bobby feels now for his daughter.
Subjects: Teen Pregnancy, Teen Father, African Americans

PRINTZ HONOR BOOKS

DONNELLY, JENNIFER. *A Northern Light*. Harcourt.
  Accepted at Barnard College, Mattie's torn between her desire to attend and her family's need for help on the farm, until a less-than-loving suitor coupled with a murder help her decide.
Subjects: Adirondack Mountains, Murder, Historical Fiction

FROST, HELEN. *Keesha's House*. Farrar, Straus & Giroux.
  Sestinas and sonnets tell the stories of teens in trouble who are able to stay in "Keesha's House," where they find safety and an extended family.
Subjects: Family, Poetry, Novel in Verse, Runaways

GOING, K. L. *Fat Kid Rules the World*. Putnam.
  Saved from suicide by thin guitarist Curt, obese Troy becomes the drummer in Curt's punk rock band, though he's never had a music lesson.
Subjects: Musician, Obesity, Drug Abuse, Depression (Mental)

MACKLER, CAROLYN. *The Earth, My Butt, and Other Big Round Things*. Candlewick.
  As the less-than-perfect child in a family of superstars, Virginia gradually loses weight, develops her own persona, and stands up for herself.
Subjects: Family, Brothers and Sisters, Body Image, Self Esteem

2003 Prizes

PRINTZ WINNER

CHAMBERS, AIDAN. *Postcards from No Man's Land*. Dutton/Penguin.
Searching for the grave of his grandfather killed during World War II, Jacob meets the woman who cared for him, and learns about love, family secrets, and his own identity.
Subjects: Historical Fiction, Holland, World War II, Family

PRINTZ HONOR BOOKS

FARMER, NANCY. *The House of the Scorpion*. Atheneum/Richard Jackson Books.
Clone of a 140-year-old drug lord, Matt sees the evils of drug harvesting in his country and at the first opportunity evicts the wrongdoers.
Subjects: Science Fiction, Cloning

FREYMANN-WEYR, GARRET. *My Heartbeat*. Houghton Mifflin.
The close-knit trio of Ellen, her brother Link, and his best friend James begins to fall apart when Ellen asks if Link and James are a couple.
Subjects: Family, Friendship, Brothers and Sisters, Gay Teens

GANTOS, JACK. *Hole in My Life*. Farrar, Straus & Giroux. **NF**
Involved in a drug scam, 20-year-old Gantos spends a year in a medium security prison where he hones his writing skills.
Subjects: Memoir, Authors, Ex Convict

2002 Prizes

PRINTZ WINNER

NA, AN. *A Step from Heaven*. Front Street.
Caught between two worlds, Young Ju struggles to be a "true" American while her parents expect her to retain the family's Korean heritage.
Subjects: Korean Americans, Family, Immigrants

PRINTZ HONOR BOOKS

DICKINSON, PETER. *The Ropemaker*. Delacorte Press.
When the protective magic unravels along the Valley's northern and southern boundaries, it's up to the powerful Ropemaker and young Tilja to restore the Valley's security.
Subjects: Fantasy, Quest, Journey

GREENBERG, JAN, ED. *Heart to Heart: New Poems Inspired by Twentieth-Century American Art*. Abrams. **NF**
This fascinating amalgamation of art and verse results from 43 poets choosing a piece of modern art and then describing it in lyrical form.
Subjects: Poetry, American Art

LYNCH, CHRIS. *Freewill*. HarperCollins.
Will wonders if he's the "carrier pigeon of death" when his striking wooden sculptures turn up near the bodies of dead teenagers.
Subjects: Death, Teen Suicide, Mystery, Grief

WOLFF, VIRGINIA EUWER. *True Believer*. Atheneum.
LaVaughn is on track to attend college and escape the projects, until her cute friend Jody moves back to the neighborhood.
Subjects: Novel in Verse, African Americans, Poverty, Friends, New York

2001 Prizes

PRINTZ WINNER

ALMOND, DAVID. *Kit's Wilderness*. Delacorte Press.
Spurred by his grandfather's tales about the coal miners in his family, Kit explores the underground mines in a too-real game of death.
Subjects: Family, Mining, Ghosts, Grandfathers, England

PRINTZ HONOR BOOKS

COMAN, CAROLYN. *Many Stones*. Front Street.
Estranged from her dad, Berry consents to travel with him to South Africa to attend a memorial service for her murdered older sister.
Subjects: South Africa, Death, Family, Fathers and Daughters

PLUM-UCCI, CAROL. *The Body of Christopher Creed*. Harcourt.
Misfit Chris Creed disappears and no one seems to really care until a popular classmate initiates a search for him.
Subjects: High School, Missing Persons

RENNISON, LOUISE. *Angus, Thongs, and Full Frontal Snogging: Confessions of Georgia Nicolson*. HarperCollins.
Georgia's diary is filled with hilarious details of a stuffed olive costume; her wacky, vicious cat Angus; and her obsession with snogging the "sex god" Robbie.
Subjects: Diary, Humor, England

TRUEMAN, TERRY. *Stuck in Neutral*. HarperCollins.
Cerebral palsied teen Shawn wishes he could tell his dad how much he wants to live, but he can't speak or control his body and hopes his dad's pity doesn't lead to euthanasia.
Subjects: Cerebral Palsy, Euthanasia, Family

2000 Prizes

PRINTZ WINNER

MYERS, WALTER DEAN. *Monster*. HarperCollins.
Sixteen-year-old Steve Harmon isn't sure whether or not he's a monster as he

describes his inadvertent involvement with a murder through the format of a movie script.

Subjects: Trials, Prison, Imprisoned Teens, African Americans, Screenplays

PRINTZ HONOR BOOKS

ALMOND, DAVID. *Skellig.* Delacorte Press.
   Neither Michael nor his neighbor Mina knows who or what the strange, winged Skellig is, but they don't care when he heals Michael's baby sister.
Subjects: Family, England, Angels

ANDERSON, LAURIE HALSE. *Speak.* Farrar, Straus & Giroux.
   After she calls the police at a before-school party, Melinda doesn't tell anyone why and is snubbed and harassed by her classmates, until the rapist threatens her again.
Subjects: High School, Rape

WITTLINGER, ELLEN. *Hard Love.* Simon & Schuster Books for Young Readers.
   John thinks he's found love in Marisol, who writes his favorite zine, only to be heartbroken when she tells him she's a lesbian.
Subjects: Friendship, Zines, Gay Teens

The Printz Awards Acceptance Speeches

Gene Luen Yang, American Born Chinese, 2007 Printz Winner

The power of images, the lineage of racism toward Asian Americans, and the coolness of graphic novels are themes in Gene Yang's acceptance speech for the 2007 Printz Award for his graphic novel American Born Chinese.

I've had a pretty amazing year. And really, that's an understatement. Two years ago, I photocopied and stapled individual chapters of *American Born Chinese* to sell by the dozen at comic book conventions, usually to personal friends or my mom. Today, I'm standing here in front of you.

Along the way from there to here, I've had the privilege of talking to many, many librarians and teachers about why graphic novels belong in our libraries and classrooms. Without exception, my message has been met with unbridled enthusiasm. There's no doubt about it. Librarians love graphic novels.

This past March, however, while I was still enjoying the afterglow of the Printz committee phone call, I began having serious self-doubts. I thought back to an incident from a few years ago when one of my students, an aspiring rap musician, gave me a copy of his album. I brought it home and played it. Though I found most of it incomprehensible, I thought it had a good beat. The next day in class I told him I liked it, and immediately his friend remarked, "Dude, Mr. Yang is a TEACHER. If he likes it, it must kinda suck."

This past March, after reflecting on this and many other similar experiences, I came to the slow realization that we adults who work with teenagers—we teachers and librarians—simply are not that cool. And really, the cooler we try to be, the more uncool we become. If you doubt me, try wearing a backward baseball cap and sagging, extra-large jeans to work some time and take a good, hard look at the faces of the teenagers you serve. You will not find admiration, I assure you.

I began to wonder: By going from library to library and school to school evangelizing librarians and teachers on the virtues of graphic novels, was I robbing comics of their cool? Would a teenager stop reading graphic novels as soon as her classroom teacher or local librarian suggested that she start reading them for her own educational benefit?

Then a month later, something happened that completely shifted my perspective. MySpace.com honored *American Born Chinese* with the dubious distinction of being their April 2007 featured book. What followed was a furious online discussion about my graphic novel among MySpace users. Although there were occasional nuggets of wisdom, the vast majority of the posts made me regret ever putting my inking brush to paper. Let me share some examples with you.

Post #1: Funnay. this book looks totally awesome. I know ppl who pee in Cokes and eat dead cats. Ba-haha

Post #2: RACIST BOOK. repost if u got any AzN pride. its practically racist against AzNz, even the dude's name is CHINK-kee and all dat s___. go to dis site and Place Bad comments, Destroy this son of a b____ book! Destroy it! Destroy it! Racist son of a b____ book!

Post #3: Shut up. its funny. leave it alone. ur mad cuz u aren't funny. ur just asian and not funny. Funny asians are better

Post #4: I think its funny hes making fun of chinks

Post #5: Heh. people still read books?

Before I went and burned my drawing table, I decided to compare these posts to posts from other online discussions on *American Born Chinese*. These other discussions took place on the Web sites of libraries and schools, and were guided by librarians and teachers. A few examples:

Post #1: I had heard about stereotypes, but never really fully understood them. This book has taught me to at least get a little grasp on the pain and hurt that stereotypes can really cause.

Post #2: It is important to know everything about yourself. . . . It's important because knowing yourself allows you to see more clearly what you want, who you consider as friends, where you want to go, how you want to live, and what you really care about. That stuff matters.

Post #3: Sometimes we choose to give up certain values or things that we believe in to get to a certain position. Part of who you are may get lost. . . . But you can always choose to get your soul back.

Post #4: [I] didn't want to be a person who had ADHD. I wanted to be normal and I kept trying to find a way to do it, I searched for a few years, but couldn't find a way to do it. Finally, I guess I just had to accept just who and what I was. Unfortunately, this urge still comes to me once in a great while.

Afterward, I had an epiphany. In a data-rich society like twenty-first-century America, we need information experts to prevent complex ideas from condensing into polarized, essentially meaningless sound bytes. We need these experts to teach us to sort good information from bad. We need them to save us from being drowned by the torrents of media we create. We need them to model for us how to think about what we read and watch and listen to. In short, my epiphany can be summed up like this: You librarians are all that stand in the way of the entire world turning into one big, no-holds-barred MySpace discussion board.

I suddenly appreciated how lucky I am to be able to count librarians among the most ardent supporters of *American Born Chinese*. My Cousin Chin-Kee character, especially, has the potential to be reduced to nothing more than a YouTube video clip in the mind of the reader. Now, it's okay for you to find him funny, but I want you to laugh at him with a knot in your stomach. Without at least a passing knowledge of Chin-Kee's historical roots, a young reader might not develop that knot.

To empower you to make knots in the stomachs of teenagers across the nation, I'd like to take some time now to deconstruct the Cousin Chin-Kee character with you. Chin-Kee stars in one of the three storylines in *American Born Chinese*.

With Chin-Kee, I attempt to tie today's popular images of Asians and Asian-Americans with the more overtly racist imagery prevalent in the late 1800s and early 1900s.

[*Mr. Yang showed a cartoon from the nineteenth century in a PowerPoint presentation at the awards reception.*] Here is a political cartoon from the 1880s, around the time the Chinese Exclusion Act was enacted.

Cartoons like this sanctioned discrimination and violence against early Asian-American communities. It is from here that Chin-Kee got his outfit and hair style.

My next example shares something in common with one of my favorite spandexed crime-fighters. Batman began in a comic book series called *Detective*

Comics, DC Comics' flagship title. Few people know, however, that *Detective Comics* did not begin with Batman. In fact, twenty-six issues of the series were published before Batman reared his brooding, pointy-eared head. The inaugural issue of *Detective Comics* featured a character much more familiar and marketable to comic book readers in the 1930s.

[*Mr. Yang showed an image of a villain from a 1930s comic book in a PowerPoint presentation at the awards reception.*] This is Ching Lung, a cheap Fu Manchu knock-off. From him Chin-Kee inherited his leering eyes and menacing slouch.

Those are the origins of Chin-Kee's appearance. One of Chin-Kee's most over-the-top lines is a word-for-word quotation from a political cartoon by an award-winning, nationally syndicated cartoonist. In a lunchroom scene in the sixth chapter of *American Born Chinese*, Chin-Kee offers Danny a bite of his "crispy fried cat gizzards with noodles." On April 9, 2001, in response to the Chinese spy plane crisis, American political cartoonist Pat Oliphant drew a six panel strip depicting Uncle Sam's visit to a Chinese restaurant, where he is served "crispy fried cat gizzards with noodles" by a slant-eyed, bucktoothed waiter.

Chin-Kee's lust for buxom American girls mirrors that of Long Duc Dong, Oriental comic relief in John Hughes's 1984 film *Sixteen Candles*. Most Asian-American men of my generation can vividly recall the sting of this character. In a strip drawn for *Giant Robot* magazine, Adrian Tomine, a fellow 30-something Asian-American cartoonist, recounts his phone interview with Gedde Watanabe, the actor who portrayed Long Duc Dong. Tomine doesn't just speak for himself when he ends the strip with an emphatic, "I hate that f———ing guy!"

Since the Civil Rights Movement in the 1960s, America has generally acknowledged that Fu Manchu and other historical caricatures of Asians and Asian-Americans are racist. But what do we make of modern-day stereotypes? Often these are treated as little more than impolite jokes. After all, Asians and Asian-Americans are largely seen as successful in American society.

Images, however, have power. And images have history. Today's depictions of Asians and Asian-Americans rest on a tradition. They draw on visual cues and short-hands already established in the mind of the audience. When we encounter John Hughes's Long Duc Dong or Pat Oliphant's Chinese waiter, we must remember who their grandfathers are. And we must ensure that the next generation does the same.

Getting the next generation to read and watch and listen with all their minds and all their hearts is no small task. Generation Next is constantly tempted to communicate through ten-letter text messages, make snap judgments based on two-minute video clips, and understand the world through a rotating set of Yahoo homepage headlines, all the while having more information at their fingertips than was available to all previous generations combined. Whether you realized it or not, when you got your librarian's degree and chose to work with teenagers, you enlisted yourself in the front lines of this struggle.

So am I robbing graphic novels of all their cool by this very act of presenting to a group of librarians? That really isn't the right question. Instead I should ask, can graphic novels—and all young adult literature, really—nurture thought, passion, and understanding within our young people? I believe the answer is yes, as long as librarians are at their side, encouraging them to not just laugh at the funny scenes and cry at the sad ones but examine what's behind their laughter and their tears.

I'd like to end by extending my gratitude to the people who made this possible. One does not go from photocopying and stapling comics by hand to making speeches in front of audiences like this one all by himself. First, I thank God for the His many blessings upon me and my family. I thank my wife for her infinite patience and love, and my two children for just being cute. I thank my parents for instilling in me a love of stories, and my brother for sharing in the habit of comic book collecting.

To my fellow cartoonists, especially those in the Bay Area alternative comics scene, and most especially Derek Kirk Kim and Lark Pien, thank you for inspiring me to be a better storyteller, for opening doors, and for partnering with me in so many ways. To Mark Siegel, Simon Boughton, Lauren Wohl, Gina Gagliano, Danica Novgorodoff, Kat Kopit and the rest of the First Second team, thank you for your vision, your passion for excellence, and your elbow grease. I am cannot tell you how lucky I am to be published by such an amazing outfit. To my agent Judy Hansen, thank you for reading and explaining to me all that fine print I find so tedious.

And finally, I thank all of you here at the Young Adult Library Services Association. Thank you for the honor of this award. Thank you for your enthusiastic support of my graphic novel. And thank you for developing the intelligent, passionate, insightful readership for whom it is such a pleasure to write and draw.

John Green, Looking for Alaska, 2006 Printz Winner

John Green describes his early acquaintance with the Printz Awards and asserts his dedication to writing for teens in his acceptance speech for the 2006 Printz Award winning Looking for Alaska.

I have either read or heard every Printz acceptance speech ever given, and so before I even say a proper thank you, I'd like to begin by asking you all to please lower your expectations. I have been pretty terrified of public speaking ever since I broke down in tears after losing the Audubon Park Elementary School oration contest to Kelsey Durkin on account of how she gesticulated more than I did. So anyway, I cannot promise a good speech. But I am going to gesticulate like crazy.

I recently read in a book about speech-giving that you should right at the outset subtly outline the arguments of your entire speech, so allow me to subtly do that right now:

First, I am going to make the bold and controversial assertion that librarians are wonderful and I love them. And in doing so, I will hopefully say a little something about *Looking for Alaska*. Although not too much, because I'm not that good at talking about the book. Whenever people ask me what *Alaska* is about, I—and this is completely true—say that it is a book about some kids at boarding school.

Then, after a lot of that, I am going to talk about my editor and my family. The main argument here—and again, this will be a provocative position to take—will be that I have the best editor, and also the best family, but I'm going to try to make that argument without offending other editors and other families. This part may include a subtle jab at the publishing business, but it will be very subtle, indeed.

Finally, I will try to patch things up with the publishing business while engaging in more librarian-praising, and then I will quote Faulkner.

But let us begin with librarians, and how wonderful they are. You may have noticed that every time a young adult author gets within shouting distance of one or more librarians, the author will start babbling on about how much s/he loves librarians, and how great librarians are, and how the very fabric of our nation would come apart at the seams were it not for librarians. YA authors talk about librarians the way that Republicans talk about rich people, and for the very same reason: We need you. You invented this thing—not just this award but the entire concept behind it. The very idea of *literature* written and published for teenagers is an idea born and nurtured in the world of librarianship. For many years now, librarians have been making courageous collection decisions as part of their service to teenagers. And by putting high-quality books in their collections, and by getting those books to kids, who sometimes end up loving a book enough to buy it, librarians have pushed publishers toward a broader and deeper understanding of what it means to write for teenagers. Mike Printz was one such librarian. His is an extraordinarily rich legacy. I never knew Mr. Printz, but without him and other librarians pushing this genre forward, I never could have published *Looking for Alaska* as a young adult novel. So in that sense, this award—and every Printz Award and Honor—belongs to librarians as much as it does the authors, although if it is okay with you I think I will keep it at my apartment and then if you want to see it you are welcome to come over.

I would particularly like to thank the extraordinarily accomplished librarians who served on this year's Printz committee, and the Young Adult Literature Services Association, who continue the ALA's long and storied tradition of, always and everywhere, using acronyms—and who also do so much for YA literature and YA librarians.

The idea for *Looking for Alaska* first occurred to me in the fall of 1999, when I was working as a student chaplain at a children's hospital. The way it worked was you sort of took classes and stuff during the day, and then about two days a week, you worked a 24-hour shift. We had these two beepers to keep with us during those 24-hours, and at the end of your shift, you handed the beepers off to the next chaplain. And so a couple times a week, I would sit alone in this little windowless room with these two beepers all night long. I would try to read or sleep, but mostly I just stared at the beepers and prayed they wouldn't go off. And then they'd go off.

I'd follow the beeper to some horrifically sad event—because chaplains aren't generally met with good news—and after it was over, I would go back to the room, alone with the beepers. And it was during those times that I began to think about questions of loss and guilt and forgiveness. When someone close to you dies, it's very typical to feel guilt, to feel that you should have done something. And usually, you eventually realize that there was nothing you could have done—that the feeling is irrational, born of a desire to explain the inexplicable, to imagine that there is something you can do in this mean world to save yourself and those you love.

But then sometimes, it is your fault—not because you are evil, but because you are careless and dumb and generally human—and I found myself wondering about that particular variety of suffering. So many other questions spun off from that one, but the initial question—of whether there can be hope in a world where people cannot help but be careless; a world where there is no chance of true justice—inspired *Alaska*.

But a lot of 22-year-olds have had a lot of ideas for a lot of books—and had I not left chaplaincy and landed as a temp at the *Booklist* offices, I might never have actually written the book. My job there involved a lot of retyping ISBN numbers, and so I became freakishly familiar with publishers' ISBN prefixes, which will figure into the story later, but one of my first assignments was to retype the speeches given by the 2000 Printz Award winners and honorees. It was the year that Walter Dean Myers won, and honors went to Ellen Wittlinger, Laurie Halse Anderson, and David Almond. When my boss explained to me that the Printz was this new award given for "literary excellence" in young adult literature, I thought (but thankfully did not say), "What, like for the metaphorical assertion that the *Sweet Valley High* lies in the shadow of Thoman Mann's *Magic Mountain?*" I had never read YA literature. But after retyping those speeches, I went home and read *Monster* and *Speak* and *Skellig* and *Hard Love*—all wonderful books. I realized then that my book—my as-yet-still-imaginary book—was YA literature, too.

And here is where librarians reenter the story. Because it was a librarian, Stephanie Zvirin, who gave me my first job and who gave me YA galleys she thought I might like. It was a librarian, Bill Ott, who took time away from his job as my boss's boss's boss to talk to me and treated me with respect and collegiality, even though as a 22-year-old I once remarked to him that someone who died at 50 could not be said to have died "young." It was an extraordinary magazine created for and by librarians, *Booklist*, that helped guide my reading and purchasing decisions. And it was a librarian, Ilene Cooper, who changed my life forever by making me believe that I could write the book inside my head.

Ilene Cooper was the first actual *author* I ever met, and she worked just down the hall from me. She would come over to my desk and ask me to do something just like a normal boss, except she wasn't a normal boss, because she *wrote books*. Ilene and I quickly became friends, because it is pretty rare in this life that one hypochondriac interested in the historical Jesus, Catholic saints, pretzels, the vast right-wing conspiracy, books, and white wine meets another. And one day I mentioned to Ilene that I wanted to write a book. She said the idea sounded promising, although I doubt she figured she'd one day have to recuse herself from a committee over it. Ilene gave me a deadline: April 15, 2001.

When that deadline passed, I'd written ten horrible pages. I'd read you a selection from those pages, except various members of the Printz Committee might rush the stage and take back this award. The central problem was that I couldn't find a structure to tell the story. And then September 11th happened, and that night I was alone in my apartment again and everyone on TV kept talking about how we'd see the world in terms of before 9/11 and after it. And I thought about how all time is measured that way—before and after the birth of Christ for Christians; before and after the *hijrah* for Muslims. This, I realized, is how I would tell my story. A year later, the manuscript was sent to Dutton.

Okay, so this is where the knowledge of ISBN prefixes reenters the story. Five months and seventeen days after sending the manuscript, Dutton called and offered to publish *Looking for Alaska*. And literally, my first thought was, "Oh. My. God. I'm going to be a zero dash five-two-five dash!"

And how lucky I have been to be a 0–525–. Dutton's publisher, Stephanie Owens-Lurie, has done so much to support this book, as has Doug Whiteman at Penguin. The world of children's publishing is increasingly dominated by blockbuster deals and mega-hits—and no, that's not the subtle jab at the publishing industry; that's still coming—but Penguin took a small book with the dreaded "questionable content" and they worked their butts off to get *Alaska* to readers, and I am so grateful for it.

But the very best facet of being a 0–525– is Julie Strauss-Gabel, my incomparable editor. In the contemporary world of YA publishing—and here's your subtle jab—far, far too many books are acquired and then published after only cursory revision because there is so much pressure to churn out titles.

That might have happened to me, and I certainly wouldn't be here if it had. But instead, I ended up with Julie Strauss-Gabel, who literally spent *years* working on *Looking for Alaska*. Fewer than half the words in the acquired manuscript appeared in the final book. We talked about *Alaska* at 2:00 a.m. on instant messenger; she sent me editorial letters longer than some Newbery winners; and when I felt like we'd done enough work, she pushed me still further. I continue to be inspired by her dedication to the craft of editing and her genuine belief in the importance of creating good books for young people. *Looking for Alaska* is a collaboration between myself and Julie, and I am proud to share this award with her.

There's one more collaborator who needs to be mentioned here, and that is my wife, Sarah. Sarah and I attended the same high school—a place that bears a stunning physical resemblance to Culver Creek Prep—but we never knew each other until just after I began revising *Alaska* in earnest. So much of her, and so many of her stories, went into this book. Alaska says one thing in particular that I stole directly from Sarah: On our very first date, Sarah said, "Imagining the future is a kind of nostalgia." So I want to thank you, Sarah, for that line, for making each day of my life fun and invigorating, and for agreeing to marry such a nostalgic guy.

I would also like to thank my parents and my brother, Hank. I had the astonishing good fortune of having my parents by my side when the Printz committee called to tell me about this award. I have an extraordinarily kind and funny and supportive family—in terms of their goodness, they are possibly even better than librarians—and I'm so glad to have my mom and dad here tonight. My greatest ambition in life is to make them proud.

I am often asked whether I wrote *Looking for Alaska* for teenagers, or whether I intended it to be a novel for adults and was just steered to a YA publisher. The answer is that I wrote it for teenagers, and my next novel is written for teenagers, and that I intend to write novels for teenagers as long as I am allowed to do so—although, to steal a line from Laurie Halse Anderson, I am really happy that the 12 adults sitting over there liked it, too. Writing for kids is the only kind of writing I know how to do that I feel is halfway noble. In his Nobel Prize Acceptance Speech, William Faulkner said, "the poet's voice need not merely be the record of man, it can be one of the props, one of the pillars that help him to endure and prevail." This is precisely why I write for young adults, and I think it's why most people in the business do what they do. When you are a teenager, you discover that life is messy. Life is defined by ambiguity and confusion and unfairness and a pervasive randomness. It is in adolescence that you realize you are not safe, not in any sense the word, and that you never will be.

When I was a teenager, I remember reading a book by the sociologist Peter Berger in which he said, "The difference between dogs and people is that dogs know how to be dogs." This is what we do as teenagers, and forever after: we try to figure out how to be people. I like writing for teenagers because they are still trying to figure out how to be people in unself-conscious, forthright ways—because they are still open to the idea that a single book might change their understanding of how to be a person. It is my fervent hope that, at least for some teenagers, books can play a role in helping them navigate the labyrinth—that books can help show us how to choose the awful pain of love over the strange comfort of destruction, that books can be a pillar to help us endure and prevail.

I realize those are some rather grand sentiments, particularly coming from a guy whose first novel features a lot of jokes about peeing. But to quote Faulkner just one last time, I believe in the importance of writing "of the heart rather than of the glands." I really hope, that in some small way, my books will help teenagers to endure and prevail. But I know that your work does. So again: Thank you.

Meg Rosoff, How I Live Now, *2005 Printz Winner*

In her acceptance speech for the 2005 Printz award for her winning novel, How I Live Now, *Meg Rosoff talks about a career of different jobs in publishing and advertising and the path that led her to writing her own books.*

I am so very grateful to be here today. So grateful, that out of my deep respect for the ALA, I sat down to write a talk entitled "Intellectual Development and The American Teenager: How Important Are Libraries Really?"

Unfortunately, I didn't know the answer.

So I figured I'd stick to what I know (which is remarkably little, given that I've spent the majority of my working life in advertising) and try to describe the serpentine path that got me here today, aged 48, in Chicago, accepting the Printz Prize for my first novel from a group of amazing librarians who seem to have cheerfully ignored the fact that underage sex and world war three are not the sort of subjects that are supposed to win young adult book prizes.

My experience suggests that careers do not always arise from a deep sense of destiny. My eight-year-old daughter, for instance, was set on a career in veterinary medicine until she discovered she would have to put her hand up a cow's bottom. Now she wants to be a penguin feeder at the zoo, which pleases me, as I hear the exams are a lot easier.

Thanks to Walter Farley, my first career ambition was to own a racing stable. Thanks to Ian Fleming and Louise Fitzhugh, my next was to be a spy. Reality was pretty sobering when the time came to get a job, and along with every other bookish girl with a degree in English Literature, it was not just any job, but The Publishing Job. My first publishing job was at a grim academic publisher in downtown Manhattan where I (and four or five girls almost identical to me in every way) edited a series of academic journals with names like *Personality Disorder Monthly*, while our sociopath of a managing editor sat, feet up, smoking cigars and reading *Playboy* all day. I lasted an impressive eight months.

At my next job, I diligently worked 50-hour weeks accomplishing absolutely nothing at all, until the day my boss teetered into my office after too many martinis, straightened his toupee, and suggested I do nothing at all at home from now on.

There followed two years at Time Inc., where I was known affectionately as the "surly minion," but even the lowest of the low had unlimited expense accounts and our main daily challenge was how to spend it all.

And then one day, I was offered a job in advertising. This was the Faustian moment of my young adulthood, the moment that should have caused me to look deep into the darkest recesses of my soul and question my morals, my goals, my values. Instead—and I am not proud of this—I thought it sounded like fun, so I took the 40 percent raise and moved crosstown to Madison Avenue that same week.

There followed 15 years in a succession of ad agency jobs, most of which I departed under a cloud—which was particularly insulting given how little intelligence it takes to write ads. During this time, I channeled most of my creative energy into elaborate escape fantasies. I would join the Peace Corps. Open a bakery. I wrote to trend-forecaster Faith Popcorn begging for a job, despite my utter lack of ability to forecast trends. I spent four months as deputy press secretary for the Democrats in New York State, having been offered the job based on my ability to write a coherent press release, a skill no one else in the press office appeared to possess. We didn't win the election, though I don't think it was my fault.

In 1989 I moved to London, refashioned my portfolio, and landed my first English ad agency job—reporting to a capriciously sadistic creative director who spent most of the working day scribbling his memoirs. I lasted two years, but it felt like twenty.

During the next six months, I wrote a guidebook to London for a small American publisher. Researching all of London proved exhausting, and I could never solve the mystery of why anyone would visit Madame Tussauds, much less queue for hours in the rain to visit Madame Tussauds. Evidence that I lacked the common touch continued to mount.

I pitched a weekly column to the features editor of the *Evening Standard* magazine. I approached the newly created Channel Five, clutching a thick sheaf of subtle and intelligent programming ideas that were rejected in favor of topless darts.

By this time, I'd been fired from yet another advertising job. Explanations were thin on the ground, but my art director suggested it had to with insubordination of an extremely high order and a general aura of contempt for my chosen profession, and was I planning to continue in this general mode? At which point, in a sudden flash of the blindingly obvious, I realized that advertising might not be for me.

By the time I reached this stunning epiphany, I was 42 and figured it might be fun to dedicate myself to another challenge, like leaving a job of my own volition. So I set my sights on something easier than selling instant coffee to housewives in Lower Codswallop upon Avon and decided to write a novel, knowing of course that you couldn't just Write A Novel, and especially that you couldn't make a living doing it.

Everyone always said write what you know, so I started with a picture book featuring four dirty, smelly, bad-tempered wild boars with no respect for authority, and within a month, my illustrator and I were involved in an auction for the rights in New York. The agent who agreed to take on the boars was not particularly interested in picture books, but in an act of extraordinary faith, set her sights on the as-yet-imaginary novel.

Sitting down to write *How I Live Now*, I was heavily motivated by a desire to impress my new agent, though having been fired by so many smug bastards in trendy suits over the years, my main motive was revenge. I'd like to say, having received advances and even a few prizes on both sides of the Atlantic, with my first novel translated into 21 languages (including Latvian and Catalan) that I've mellowed, that I wish my ex-colleagues well, am anxious to let bygones be bygones, that I open my arms wide and invite them to join me in my happiness. But that would be a big fat lie.

Instead, I say to them now: HA. Who gets to sit home and eat toast and talk on the phone all day, and who has to get up at 5:00 a.m. to travel nine hours by train to sell new improved panty liner campaign? But to be fair, I did learn a lot from those years in advertising. I learned to edit my prose ruthlessly. And I learned that explaining to your boss that he is dull, talentless, and laughably unattractive often ends in dismissal.

Anyway, in the end, I wrote *How I Live Now* very quickly. Originally titled *Life During Wartime* after a Talking Head's song, it took on a life of its own almost from the start, and I delivered the first draft in about three months. There was an auction in the UK. A bigger one in the U.S., and suddenly, I was a writer. I phoned my mother. "Whatever you do, don't leave your job," she advised. My mother is a wise and astute person, and I've always taken her advice, though rarely in the spirit that she intends. I quit the next day.

And now, almost two years later, the first question everyone asks is: Don't you wish you'd done it sooner?

And the obvious answer is, no.

If I'd written my first novel 20 years ago, I'd probably still be trying to get it published today. It would have emerged tortured, humorless, and pretentious; a thinly disguised autobiography attracting rejection after rejection, leading to permanent psychological and emotional scarring. I would by now be living with my eleven children in an old Buick under the railway bridge, an embittered failure, drinking gin for breakfast and having nightmares in which I write *The Da Vinci Code* but forget to get it published.

So it's worth reporting that becoming a writer late in life is not a bad thing. It makes your parents very happy for one thing, far happier than if you'd done it right away and let them relax and take it for granted. And for another thing, when you actually get that amazing phone call in deepest North London on a dark winter night from a group of wonderful, cheering librarians on a speaker phone and they tell you you've won the Printz prize, your eyes fill with tears partly because you're so incredibly moved that they chose your book, and partly because you're so incredibly thrilled that you will never have to work in advertising again.

Angela Johnson, The First Part Last, 2004 Printz Winner

Expressing the truth her characters need to tell is one of the creative challenges discussed by Angela Johnson, Printz winner in 2004 for her novel about a single teenage father raising his daughter, The First Part Last.

Good evening.

It is an honor to be with you here tonight as only the fifth winner of the Michael L. Printz Award. By creating this separate category, you have recognized those of us who write about the world of the young adult, a time when our characters are wrestling between the world of childhood with its first awakening to life's possibilities—and the inevitability of becoming an adult, when choices often bring a lifetime of consequences.

The first Printz awards were given at the beginning of a new century—with a fresh appreciation that while some things remain the same, we have also managed to create some complications. Certainly no librarian in 1900 could have imagined the libraries we are now building. And aren't we happy that those who predicted the death of the books we actually hold in our hands are still wrong.

People describe this period of time in which we live as being most changed by technology. As someone who bought her first computer less than a year ago, I understand a little of what they mean. As a woman who used to spend her nights wandering around the house quietly, I now find myself surfing the net ordering too many books or CDs online. The young slip into this world as if they were born to it. And they were. But while technology may make it easier to more quickly access knowledge, machines still don't change the challenges of the teenage heart. First-time love, friendships, death, sex, drugs and alcohol, racism, exclusion from their peers, or a body that seems to have a life of its own, growing in directions so unfamiliar the person who was in the mirror yesterday—is a stranger today.

No technology can change that. No machine has made the journey less predictable. When our teens flops down on the floor of their room and find the paper they never found for 4th period English or the clothes they have been wearing too long, they are always wrestling in a world of feuding emotions and time.

Most of us at one point entered into that tunnel of adolescence that creates the illusion that anyone over the age of 25 is a mystery. Our parents seemed either distant, too involved with us, or, quite frankly, more stupid with each passing day. But how painful to be young and searching through the mysteries and vagaries of the human heart.

For me, to write the characters in YA fiction the childhood of picture books and middle readers, become as distant as the moon. What can I bring to writing for this world? For me it is simple. The comfort of Truth. Not just the truth that I'd prefer, but the truth of life in all its variations of a teen experience. I know what a comfort it is to find out who you are. I know the pain of wondering if anyone else will ever know it. And on days like this, I know the pleasure and pride that someone else knows me too. As a young woman I wrote poetry and dreamed of that time five, ten, or twenty years down the road when I might have mastered my craft enough to call myself a writer.

I quickly learned that being a writer is not just the love of writing, but the business of being a writer. As I never intended to write *The First Part Last* I had to come to understand that sometimes the muse is not always in control, but that others vision are sometimes clearer than your own, e.g., my editor who asked if there was indeed a story about Bobby I had to tell.

But now I had to open my imagination up to explore how this young man came to be raising this baby by himself. I knew Bobby loved Feather, felt that the first time I wrote about him. But how did he get to Ohio? Where was the mother of this baby? His parents? How did his journey take him to teen fatherhood?

The gifted actress Ruby Dee once said that "the greatest gift is not being afraid to question." In writing *The First Part Last* I had nothing but questions. But after I had put off the writing as long as I could, figuring out how many new places in my house I could discover to clean, or whether it wasn't a good day to weed that garden that was growing up onto my porch, I would eventually have to ask and answer those questions. They would be easy. They just wouldn't be just MY answers. They had to be Bobby's.

The idea of wanting to protect young people from life's realities is like trying to hold back time. You may fly in a plane to the west so that you can go backward an hour, two, even twelve hours, but eventually, today will become tomorrow. Trying to write novels in which pain, suffering, sex, accidents, mistakes, joy, love, death, don't happen, is just putting your head into the sand so deeply you might as well believe—as we did when we were children—that eventually you'd come out the other side of the earth. I find writing for teens demands writing a truth. Not the truth mind you . . . a truth.

If I had written *The First Part Last* on my truth and personal philosophy, Bobby would NOT be raising a baby at all. Teen sex, birth control, abortion, adoption are all options and truth for young people. Bobby's truth would not be mine, but as a writer I can't always be a mouthpiece for my own personal agendas (although I struggle against it constantly).

Charles Dickens said, "it was the season of Light, it was the season of Darkness, it was the spring of hope, it was the winter of despair, we had everything before us, we had nothing before us, we were all going direct to Heaven, we were all going direct the other way. . . ." That's what I had to write about. The challenge for me as a writer—as an artist—was crawling inside the skin of Bobby, Nia, his mother, father, and everyone else that cares about him. To understand his fears, his passion, his moment of crossing over from a boy to a father and make it real. Not my world—his world. Not my view, but his reality.

When a character says, "I'm here," I must listen. I have to listen to Bobby say, "Think about what I'm doing here with this baby. I'm a young teenage father. The world sees me as just another black boy who's got a baby. I want to be a man, a father. I'm growing up before your eyes if you let me." So when my ears start listening, my mouth starts watering, my heart starts beating, and if I'm very, very lucky, it all becomes the eyes and ears and heart of an incredible character who will live on. His name could be Bobby and his baby Feather. A spirit so bright it almost makes the weight of being a father light enough to bear without buckling.

This was a real challenge, but I was handed a gift—I knew the end of the story, I just didn't know how he would meet that end. In this case, I had to create his world—the world of a teenage boy in the middle of New York City who thought he had the world in his hands until a different life started happening. But as usual, life does not follow rules. It makes demands. It kicks the bottom out of dreams. It says you better be ready to rewrite your life because you just changed direction.

If as a writer I follow the path that is mindful it will take me to that which is truthful, not necessarily convenient or uplifting. In that YA literature triumphs. Life happens. It's messy and chaotic, sometimes boring and brutal. Can we celebrate and write about that which is wonderful and never do justice to the other? Shall we write about our riches and superiority and never discuss the problematic, devastating, and sad? Should we write about happy families instead of orphans and the disaffected in a world that chooses war and destruction over improved reading scores, decent housing, and social programs? Should we not write about passion, loneliness, and the exclusion of large segments of our own children from the dream? Should we wave the flag, call ourselves patriots, and exclude the amazing, ugly, and sometimes regrettable truth. . . .

The creative spirit can be beaten down. People may criticize our books, try to ban and exclude them from our schools and libraries, but they can't change the fact that they exist. They will be found and read, and if they are speaking to the lives of their audience, they won't be forgotten.

I'd like to thank The Printz Committee for their acceptance of mine and all the 2004 recipients' work. I'd like to thank my Editor Kevin Lewis for vision and my agent Barry Goldblatt for his patience and trust. And last but not least, The American Library Association for always fighting the good fight.

Good night.

Aidan Chambers, **Postcards from No Man's Land***, 2003 Printz Winner*

In a speech suffused with gratitude, Aidan Chambers, 2003 Printz Award Winner for Postcards from No Man's Land, *discusses the power teachers, librarians, and publishers have to encourage young adults to become thoughtful, literate readers.*

I revel in the exceptional honor of receiving the Michael L. Printz Award, and am grateful to the jury for their recognition. It comes at an interesting time in my career, as you can judge from the following e-mail from a 15-year-old reader.

> Mr Chambers. Our teacher made us read your book *Postcards from No Man's Land*. I now have to write about it. I was surprised to learn from your website that you are still alive. But I have also worked out that you are old enough to retire. Does this mean I will not have to read any more of your books?

I took pleasure in telling this young correspondent that I will indeed be writing more books, but comforted him by adding that it takes me so long to produce a novel that by the time the next one appears he will be too old to be made to read it in school. I also told him about the Printz Award and said how much this encouraged me to go on writing.

Apart from the encouragement of the award, however, it is also a special pleasure and a particular satisfaction for reasons I'd like to explain. There is one person and there are two institutions without which I would not have been able to write any of my books, least of all the one you are honoring today. What's more, such a person and similar institutions are essential, it seems to me, in the lives of all of us who become serious readers. I mean by "serious readers" those of us who read not merely for pastime entertainment, and not only for information, but who read for its own sake, or, as Gustav Flaubert put it, those of us who read to live.

In my case, the essential person was called Jim Osborn. He was my English teacher during my last four years in high school. Until I met him, I was the kind of reader who wanted every book to please me because it was the kind I already knew I liked. Jim taught me that the best literature requires the reader to give him or herself up to it. He taught me how to become the reader the book wanted me to be. He taught me how to be the partner of the writer, doing the pleasurable work the writer had left me to do. And he taught me how to do that with the kind of thoughtful discrimination that was sympathetic without being uncritical, and which yielded the greatest enjoyment. Jim taught me how to live as a reader.

But of course, no reader can be a reader without books to read. And that's where the two essential institutions I have in mind come into play. The first of these was the glory of a free public library service. I come from a poor family. Without the asset of a free public library I would never have had access to all of the books I knew I wanted and those Jim introduced me to. What's more, I would not have grown as a reader by the invaluable self-education of serendipity. It was while touring the shelves in my town's central library once a week during my teens that I stumbled across writers of whom I had never heard—writers with names like Balzac and Colette, Thomas Mann and Flaubert, Steinbeck and Turgenev, Virginia Woolf and Emily Dickinson, and many more.

Had my local library regarded itself as simply a warehouse of books that people already know they like—the books that are bestsellers and are often borrowed—such writers would not have been stocked. But in those days—the 1940s and '50s—the public library service in Britain regarded itself as a place where everyone could find the whole range of literature, not merely the popular and in-demand. I'm not sure we are so blessed these days, since the depredations of Philistine populism and crude market-accountancy have been applied to education and library provision. But, like it or not, it remains true that any democracy and its politicians can be judged by how vigorously supported and how well-funded is a *free* public library service. The fact is, if we want writers of many kinds, if we want to educate well, if we want a literature that is representative of all, is innovative and rich in nature, then we cannot do without the generous, cultural powerhouse of a comprehensive library service.

The second essential institution happened, in my youth, to be called Penguin Books. Every week I toured the shelves of my local public library, and every week I pored over the paperback bookshelves of my local bookshop. Like every serious reader, I wanted to own the books that mattered to me. I couldn't afford all of them—in fact I couldn't afford *any* of them—in hardback. Penguin Books were a godsend. They published almost everything I wanted at a price that allowed me to buy one or even two books a week with my meager pocket-money. They were designed with a classic simplicity that was at the same time modern. I was proud to be seen reading them.

If we want a democracy that is also literary—a democracy that provides for serious readers from the least well-off homes—then we need inexpensive editions of all our literature, the rare and the difficult as well as the easy. And we need them to be published with as much care in design and typography and printing as the most expensive of books.

Now you can see why I am so pleased to be given the Michael L. Printz Award. I am receiving an award given under the aegis of a public library system, judged by librarians with a special interest in the young and named after a school librarian. Michael Printz was a much-respected professional, who, like Jim Osborn, knew how to draw young people into literature. He could do this because he was a serious reader himself, knew literature as a whole, and the literature for young adults in particular, knew how to present books attractively and how to make sympathetic critical discrimination a pleasure it itself.

The award that bears his name is given by the American Library Association's specialists in young adult literature. These are the inheritors of the librarians who, in my hometown 50 years ago, maintained the service that nurtured me and provided the books my teacher Jim Osborn had opened up to me. Librarians deserve all the thanks, all the encouragement and all the support we can give them.

I know how hard and how rewarding the work of a school librarian is. I know because I was a school librarian myself for seven years during the 1960s. My commitment to this work is such that I am proud to tell you that a few days after I return home from this meeting I will be installed as president of the British School Library Association during our annual summer conference. I am therefore able to bring you the greetings of your colleagues in Britain.

Furthermore, *Postcards from No Man's Land*, the book you honor today, was published by Dutton, which is an imprint of Penguin Books. True, it is not yet in paperback. I hope it will be before long so that those serious young readers who, like myself at their age, cannot afford hardbacks, will be able to buy it for themselves. But that it is published by an arm of Penguin adds a personal satisfaction to my receiving this award.

The award sums up my beginnings as a reader and a writer and honors not me but those people who made it possible for me to write any books at all, among which is another person who adds another layer to the private satisfaction the award gives me. My wife, Nancy, was born and educated in the United States and is still a citizen of that country, even though she has lived in England since 1965. She began her career at the Horn Book. We married soon after she moved to England, and since 1970 has published and edited *Signal*, her own magazine about children's literature. Without her aid and support, not to mention her editorial acumen, I would certainly not have produced the books that have brought me the Carnegie Medal, the Hans Christian Andersen Award, and now the Michael L. Printz Award. Nancy supported and encouraged me through all the years before anyone else thought my books worth much notice.

So, finally, my thanks to the teachers who help us discover what we cannot discover by ourselves. My thanks to the librarians who preserve our literature, who enable readers to go beyond themselves, and who supply the needs of all our people, whether those be minorities or majorities. My thanks to the publishers who take the risk of publishing more than the narrow-minded confines of the instantly popular and the immediately profitable. And my special thanks to Nancy and those companions and editors like her who sustain authors during their unrecognized formative years.

And if I may, I'll end with some words sent to me from another young reader, this time one who was rather more enthusiastic than the young man I quoted earlier. "I like your books," she wrote, "because each one is a little part of a long life."

Thank you for honoring one of the little parts of what I hope will yet be a much longer life, even though I have reached the age when I am old enough to retire.

An Na, A Step from Heaven, 2002 Printz Winner

An Na, 2002 Printz Award Winner for her novel A Step From Heaven *about the Korean immigrant experience in America, speaks about her love of reading and her belief that everyone can and should contribute their experiences to expand the diversity of our literary and cultural heritage.*

It is an incredible honor for me to stand here before you as the third recipient of the Michael L. Printz Award. I would like to thank the members of the Printz Award Selection Committee. If they would all stand up please. These dedicated members read hundreds and hundreds of books. I don't know how you all came to choose my first novel from all the many amazing and beautiful works published every year, like the ones produced by the authors that I have the privilege to stand next to today, but I would just like to recognize and memorize these committee members' faces since I'll be coming after all of you the next time I have writer's block. Thank you for your support, your faith in my novel. You have opened doors, not only for me, but also for countless other present and future Asian-American writers.

As a first generation Korean American immigrant growing up in a mostly white suburban neighborhood in San Diego, there was so much of the world around me that I couldn't understand. Couldn't access. My parents, both struggling themselves to make sense of American culture, did not have the tools to answer my questions. But what they lacked in understanding, they made up for in wisdom. My father knew that books have always been and continue to be the path to knowledge. Even before I could read, one of the first things my father did for me was to subscribe to a book-of-the-month club. I remember clearly my first book coming in the mail, packaged in its brown cardboard wrap. It was a hefty book, a real book, a book called *A Little Princess*. I proceeded to draw all over the pages with my crayons. No pictures. No problem. I would make my own. Needless to say, someone took that book away from me and put it on a very high shelf. As they did with all the other ones that would come monthly like clockwork. I was allowed to open the box, but then the books would be put away until I could read them properly. This became a goal for me. To finally claim what was mine.

I don't remember exactly learning how to read. I remember being in class, sitting in a circle, holding those early readers about Jane and Spot, but I can't remember ever making sounds or coming to some ah-ha moment. Rather my first memory of reading is intimately connected to my first memory of being in a library. I can still recall pushing open the glass doors, taking those first tentative steps inside, my sister and brother sandwiched close behind me, my mother in the back urging us forward. After helping my mother fill out the form for a library card, we were let loose to roam among the endless rows of books. From between those magical aisles stirs my first memory of reading. Sitting cross-legged on the carpeted floor, my head cocked to one side, I sounded out title after title and pulled the books into my lap. Frog and Toad were early favorites. Then came all the Beverly Cleary and Laura Ingalls Wilder books. And as I got older, I ventured into the nonfiction and reference areas.

Books were my savior, my first love, my teachers and friends. When my parents couldn't answer my questions, when I was too embarrassed to ask my teachers and friends at school about something as silly as eggnog, I turned to books for the answer. Judy Blume got me through puberty. That tattered copy of *Forever* being passed around the room in the sixth grade had all the "good" parts dog-eared. The twins of Sweet Valley High made me feel like I was part of the in crowd or at least what it would feel like to be popular. Madeleine L'Engle sent me shooting to other time dimensions and planets. And I finally did read all those books that my father had ordered for me. I cried while reading *A Little Princess*, rooted for Old Yeller to live, and whooped right along with Dan and Ann as they hunted down that ghostly raccoon. These were my lessons in Americana. These characters and families were so different from my reality, and yet there were enough similarities so that I felt connected to these fictional lives. The parents in the books I read harbored hopes and dreams for their children just as my parents did. They nagged their kids just as much too. The protagonist often struggled with either internal or external conflicts in ways that I could understand and sympathize with. And yet, there was a gap.

Growing up, I never ran across a book that spoke directly to the kind of experiences that I went through. The painful names of racism, of knowing that your mother and father could not complete forms and documents without you, that life inside the home was so different than what was outside. I did not read books by Asian Americans or Latinos, and very few by African-American authors. Surely these books must have existed back then? I don't know. I never ran across them on my own and I didn't have a librarian point them out to me. It wasn't until college that I was introduced to ethnic literature. In fact, I took a whole class on it. Story after story about what it meant to lead a dual existence, to be stuck in between cultures, languages, expectations, priorities. These lives spoke to the particularities of my life. Where had they been all this time?

A lot has changed since I was first learning how to read. The face of America has changed. We are a more diverse nation today than we ever were before. There are more languages being spoken, more religions being practiced, more cultures and histories to be recognized. In Texas, Florida, New York, and California, the majority student population is now made up of minorities: Latinos, Asians, and African Americans among others. In California, one in every three students comes from families that do not speak English as their primary language. One in four students are in bilingual or English Learner Development classes. In some urban areas like San Francisco, Los Angeles, and San Diego, as many as 47 languages are spoken by students in these schools. That is an astonishing number. But a very real number. It is this reality that must be addressed. In our libraries and schools today, do the books we have the children read reflect the world that they live in? Reflect the diversity of experiences and languages that surround them?

Our world is changing faster than the publishing house or library or school can keep up. Yet, try we must. We must write, we must read, we must encourage, support, and honor the differences and similarities between lives. It is a slow process, and one that is often cyclical in nature. If we had more authors of color, we would have more books about their experiences. If we had more books about people of color and their experiences, then we would have more authors. If we had more awards for people of color. But then they become segregated to just a niche. If we recognized more people of color in the major awards. But maybe their book wasn't the best that year. So where does this leave us? Where must we begin? I believe we must work on all fronts.

Each ripple of change creates another ripple, touches a life, engenders a discussion, provokes action. The fact that two Korean Americans were honored this year with the highest achievement in children's literature established the Korean-American experience as a vital and integral part of this nation's history. This message of multiculturalism spoke to Korean Americans and Asian Americans all over the country, and resonated clear across the oceans to Korea. At speaking engagements, Korean mothers claim me as their own, tell me how proud they are that someone has addressed the needs and issues of their community, that Korean American children can imagine growing up to be writers. Ripple after ripple after ripple.

We can only grow richer, more knowledgeable, better informed when we recognize diversity. Librarians, teachers, parents, publishers, and writers should all be in constant dialogue with one another about how to best present this changing world to our children. There will be disagreements and heated battles, but hopefully there will also be fruitful collaborations. Together we can create books that serve as the vehicles from which a multitude of experiences and worlds can be shared.

My mother, as tired as she was every weekend, always found time to take us to the library. Sometimes she would drop us off and run errands while we were inside. Other times, she would slide back her seat, drop down the backrest, and take a nap. It was rare for my mother to come inside the library. For all that books could offer her children, they were nothing but black scratches on paper to her. My mother never had the opportunity to learn how to read English. Even now, she can only stare at the cover of my novel, skim her fingertips over the words on the pages and wait for me to tell her the story. She is not alone in her predicament. So many parents share her same story. So many parents sacrifice for the sake of their children's education, for a dream of a better future. In return, the children teach their parents what they have learned. So when we put books in the hands of children, we are not only putting them in their hands but by extension into the hands of their families and the hands of their future. Ripple after ripple after ripple.

Thank you.

Chapter 6

Reproducible Materials You Can Use to Promote These Great Reads

The following pages are intended to serve as handouts listing valuable reading material recommended by YALSA (Young Adult Library Services Association). The books are the winners from the following awards programs:

- **The Alex Winners** (1998–2008)
- **The Edwards Winners** (1991–2008)
- **The Printz Winners** (2000–2008)

Simply xerox the pages at 130–135 percent, and you will have ready-made handouts for young readers at your library. They will have enough valuable literature to choose from to keep them occupied throughout their teen years.

The Alex Winners

ALEXANDER, CAROLINE — *The Endurance: Shackleton's Legendary Antarctic Expedition* **NF** (Alex 1999)

ALMOND, STEVE — *Candyfreak: A Journey Through the Chocolate Underbelly of America* **NF** (Alex 2005)

BARRY, LYNDA — *One Hundred Demons* **NF** (Alex 2003)

BATES, JUDY FONG — *Midnight at the Dragon Café* (Alex 2006)

BEAH, ISHMAEL — *A Long Way Gone: Memoirs of a Boy Soldier* **NF** (Alex 2008)

BODANIS, DAVID — *The Secret Family: Twenty-Four Hours Inside the Mysterious Worlds of Our Minds and Bodies* **NF** (Alex 1998)

BOYLAN, JAMES FINNEY — *Getting In* (Alex 1999)

BRADLEY, JAMES AND RON POWERS — *Flags of Our Fathers* **NF** (Alex 2001)

BRADSHAW, GILLIAN — *The Sand-reckoner* (Alex 2001)

BRAGG, RICK — *All Over but the Shoutin'* **NF** (Alex 1998)

BREASHEARS, DAVID — *High Exposure: An Enduring Passion for Everest and Unforgiving Places* **NF** (Alex 2000)

BROOKS, GERALDINE — *Year of Wonders: A Novel of the Plague* (Alex 2002)

BUCKHANON, KALISHA	*Upstate* (Alex 2006)
CARD, ORSON SCOTT	*Ender's Shadow* (Alex 2000)
CARROLL, REBECCA	*Sugar in the Raw: Voices of Young Black Girls in America* **NF** (Alex 1998)
CHEVALIER, TRACY	*The Girl with a Pearl Earring* (Alex 2001)
CLARKE, BREENA	*River, Cross My Heart* (Alex 2000)
CODELL, ESME RAJI	*Educating Esme: Diary of a Teacher's First Year* **NF** (Alex 2000)
COLTON, LARRY	*Counting Coup* **NF** (Alex 2001)
CONNOLLY, JOHN	*The Book of Lost Things* (Alex 2007)
CONROY, PAT	*My Losing Season* **NF** (Alex 2003)
COOK, KARIN	*What Girls Learn* (Alex 1998)
COX, LYNN	*Swimming to Antarctica: Tales of a Long-Distance Swimmer* **NF** (Alex 2005)
DAVIS, AMANDA	*Wonder When You'll Miss Me* (Alex 2004)
DOIG, IVAN	*The Whistling Season* (Alex 2007)
DOMINICK, ANDIE	*Needles: A Memoir of Growing up with Diabetes* **NF** (Alex 1999)
D'ORSO, MICHAEL	*Eagle Blue: A Team, a Tribe and a High School Basketball Season in Arctic Alaska* **NF** (Alex 2007)
DOYLE, WILLIAM	*An American Insurrection: The Battle of Oxford Mississippi 1962* **NF** (Alex 2002)
DURHAM, DAVID ANTHONY	*Gabriel's Story* (Alex 2002)
EHRENREICH, BARBARA	*Nickel and Dimed: On (Not) Getting By in Boom-time America* **NF** (Alex 2002)
ENGER, LEIF	*Peace Like a River* (Alex 2002)
FERRIS, TIMOTHY	*Seeing in the Dark* **NF** (Alex 2003)
FFORDE, JASPER	*The Eyre Affair* (Alex 2003)
FUQUA, JONATHON SCOTT	*The Reappearance of Sam Weber* (Alex 2000)

GAIMAN, NEIL
Anansi Boys (Alex 2006)
Stardust (Alex 2000)

GALLOWAY, GREGORY
As Simple As Snow (Alex 2006)

GILSTRAP, JOHN
At All Costs (Alex 1999)

GREENLAW, LINDA
The Hungry Ocean: A Swordboat Captain's Journey **NF** (Alex 2000)

GRUEN, SARA
Water for Elephants (Alex 2007)

HADDON, MARK
The Curious Incident of the Dog in the Night-time (Alex 2004)

HALPIN, BRENDAN
Donorboy (Alex 2005)

HAMAMURA, JOHN
Color of the Sea (Alex 2007)

HAMILL, PETE
Snow in August (Alex 1998)

HART, ELVA TREVINO
Barefoot Heart: Stories of a Migrant Child **NF** (Alex 2000)

HARUF, KENT
Plainsong (Alex 2000)

HOSSEINI, KHALED
The Kite Runner (Alex 2004)

IGUULDEN, CONN
Genghis: Birth of an Empire (Alex 2008)

ISHIGURO, KAZUO
Never Let Me Go (Alex 2006)

JOERN, PAMELA CARTER
The Floor of the Sky (Alex 2007)

JONES, LLOYD
Mister Pip (Alex 2008)

JORDAN, JUNE
Soldier: A Poet's Childhood **NF** (Alex 2001)

JUNGER, SEBASTIAN
The Perfect Storm: A True Story of Men Against the Sea **NF** (Alex 1998)

KERSHEVAL, JESSE LEE
Space: A Memoir **NF** (Alex 1999)

KLUGER, STEVE
Last Days of Summer (Alex 1999)

KRAKAUER, JON
Into Thin Air: A Personal Account of the Mt. Everest Disaster **NF** (Alex 1998)

KRUGER, KOBIE
The Wilderness Family: At Home with Africa's Wildlife **NF** (Alex 2002)

KURSON, ROBERT	*Shadow Divers: The True Adventure of Two Americans Who Risked Everything to Solve One of the Last Mysteries of World War II* **NF** (Alex 2005)
KYLE, ARYN	*The God of Animals* (Alex 2008)
LAWSON, MARY	*Crow Lake* (Alex 2003)
LEMIRE, JEFF	*Essex County Volume I: Tales from the Farm* (Alex 2008)
LEWIS, MICHAEL	*The Blind Side: Evolution of a Game* **NF** (Alex 2007)
LUTZ, LISA	*The Spellman Files* (Alex 2008)
MALLOY, BRIAN	*The Year of Ice* (Alex 2003)
MALTMAN, THOMAS	*The Night Birds* (Alex 2008)
MARILLIER, JULIET	*Daughter of the Forest* (Alex 2001)
MARTINEZ, A. LEE	*Gil's All Fright Diner* (Alex 2006)
MEYERS, KENT	*Work of Wolves* (Alex 2005)
MITCHELL, DAVID	*Black Swan Green* (Alex 2007)
MORRISSEY, DONNA	*Kit's Law* (Alex 2002)
NIFFENEGGER, AUDREY	*The Time Traveler's Wife* (Alex 2004)
ODOM, MEL	*The Rover* (Alex 2002)
OTSUKA, JULIE	*When the Emperor Was Divine* (Alex 2003)
PACKER, ANN	*The Dive from Clausen's Pier* (Alex 2003)
PACKER, Z. Z.	*Drinking Coffee Elsewhere* (Alex 2004)
PALWICK, SUSAN	*The Necessary Beggar* (Alex 2006)
PATCHETT, ANN	*Truth and Beauty: A Friendship* **NF** (Alex 2005)
PHILBRICK, NATHANIEL	*In the Heart of the Sea: The Tragedy of the Whaleship Essex* **NF** (Alex 2001)
PICOULT, JODI	*My Sister's Keeper* (Alex 2005)
POLLY, MATTHEW	*American Shaolin: Flying Kicks, Buddhist Monks, and the Legend of Iron Crotch: An Odyssey in the New China* **NF** (Alex 2008)

PORTER, CONNIE	*Imani All Mine* (Alex 2000)
RASH, RON	*The World Made Straight* (Alex 2007)
RAWLES, NANCY	*My Jim* (Alex 2006)
REED, KIT	*Thinner Than Thou* (Alex 2005)
ROACH, MARY	*Stiff* **NF** (Alex 2004)
ROBINSON, KIM STANLEY	*Antarctica* (Alex 1999)
ROTHFUSS, PATRICK	*The Name of the Wind* (Alex 2008)
RUFF, MATT	*Bad Monkeys* (Alex 2008)
SALZMAN, MARK	*True Notebooks* **NF** (Alex 2004)
SANTIAGO, ESMERALDA	*Almost a Woman* **NF** (Alex 1999)
SATRAPI, MARJANE	*Persepolis: The Story of a Childhood* **NF** (Alex 2004)
SCHEERES, JULIA	*Jesus Land: A Memoir* **NF** (Alex 2006)
SENNA, DANZY	*Caucasia* (Alex 1999)
SETTERFIELD, DIANE	*The Thirteenth Tale* (Alex 2007)
SHEPARD, JIM	*Project X* (Alex 2005)
SHERWOOD, BEN	*The Man Who Ate the 747* (Alex 2001)
SILVERBERG, ROBERT, EDITOR	*Legends: Short Novels by the Masters of Modern Fantasy* (Alex 1999)
SOUTHGATE, MARTHA	*The Fall of Rome* (Alex 2003)
STRAUSS, DARIN	*Chang and Eng: A Novel* (Alex 2001)
SULLIVAN, ROBERT	*Rats: Observations on the History and Habitat of the City's Most Unwanted Inhabitants* **NF** (Alex 2005)
THOMAS, VELMA MAIA	*Lest We Forget: The Passage from Africa to Slavery and Emancipation* **NF** (Alex 1998)
TRICE, DAWN TURNER	*Only Twice I've Wished for Heaven* (Alex 1998)
VIJAYARAGHAVAN, VINEETA	*Motherland* (Alex 2002)
WALKER, REBECCA	*Black, White, and Jewish: Autobiography of a Shifting Self* **NF** (Alex 2002)

WALLS, JEANNETTE	*The Glass Castle: A Memoir* **NF** (Alex 2006)
WATT, ALAN	*Diamond Dogs* (Alex 2001)
WEISBERG, JOSEPH	*10th Grade* (Alex 2003)
WILLIS, CONNIE	*To Say Nothing of the Dog; or, How We Found the Bishop's Bird Stump at Last* (Alex 1998)
WINSPEAR, JACQUELINE	*Maisie Dobbs* (Alex 2004)
YATES, BART	*Leave Myself Behind* (Alex 2004)

The Edwards Winners

BLOCK, FRANCESCA LIA (2005)
Baby Be-Bop
Cherokee Bat and the Goat Guys
Missing Angel Juan
Weetzie Bat
Witch Baby

BLUME, JUDY (1996)
Forever

CARD, ORSON SCOTT (2008)
Ender's Game
Ender's Shadow

CORMIER, ROBERT (1991)
After the First Death
The Chocolate War
I Am the Cheese

CRUTCHER, CHRIS (2000)
Athletic Shorts
Chinese Handcuffs
The Crazy Horse Electric Game
Running Loose
Staying Fat for Sarah Byrnes
Stotan!

DUNCAN, LOIS (1992)

Chapters **NF**
I Know What You Did Last Summer
Killing Mr. Griffin
Ransom
Summer of Fear
The Twisted Window

GARDEN, NANCY (2003)

Annie on My Mind

HINTON, S. E. (1988)

The Outsiders
Rumble Fish
Tex
That Was Then, This Is Now

KERR, M. E. (1993)

Dinky Hocker Shoots Smack!
Gentlehands
Me Me Me Me Me **NF**
Night Kites

LE GUIN, URSULA K. (2004)

The Beginning Place
The Farthest Shore
The Left Hand of Darkness
Tehanu
The Tombs of Atuan
A Wizard of Earthsea

L'ENGLE, MADELEINE (1998)

Meet the Austins
Ring of Endless Light
A Swiftly Tilting Planet
A Wrinkle in Time

LIPSYTE, ROBERT (2001)

The Brave
The Chief

	The Contender
	One Fat Summer
Lowry, Lois **(2007)**	*The Giver*
McCaffrey, Anne **(1999)**	*Dragondrums*
	Dragonflight
	Dragonquest
	Dragonsinger
	Dragonsong
	The Ship Who Sang
	The White Dragon
Myers, Walter Dean **(1994)**	*Fallen Angels*
	Hoops
	Motown and Didi
	Scorpions
Paulsen, Gary **(1997)**	*Canyons*
	The Crossing
	Dancing Carl
	Hatchet
	Winter Room
	Woodsong
Peck, Richard **(1990)**	*Are You in the House Alone?*
	Father Figure
	The Ghost Belonged to Me
	Ghosts I Have Been
	Remembering the Good Times
	Secrets of the Shopping Mall
Voigt, Cynthia **(1995)**	*Building Blocks*
	Dicey's Song

Homecoming

Jackaroo

The Runner

A Solitary Blue

WOODSON, JACQUELINE (2006)

From the Notebooks of Melanin Sun

I Hadn't Meant to Tell You This

If You Come Softly

Lena

Miracle's Boys

ZINDEL, PAUL (2002)

The Effects of Gamma Rays on Man-in-the-Moon Marigolds: A Drama in Two Acts

My Darling, My Hamburger

The Pigman

The Pigman and Me

The Pigman's Legacy

The Printz Winners

ALMOND, DAVID	*Kit's Wilderness* (Printz Winner 2001)
	Skellig (Printz Honor 2000)
ANDERSON, LAURIE HALSE	*Speak* (Printz Honor 2000)
ANDERSON, M. T.	*The Astonishing Life of Octavian Nothing, Traitor to the Nation, Volume 1: The Pox Party* (Printz Honor 2007)
CHAMBERS, AIDAN	*Postcards from No Man's Land* (Printz Winner 2003)
CLARKE, JUDITH	*One Whole and Perfect Day* (Printz Honor 2008)
COMAN, CAROLYN	*Many Stones* (Printz Honor 2001)
DICKINSON, PETER	*The Ropemaker* (Printz Honor 2002)
DONNELLY, JENNIFER	*A Northern Light* (Printz Honor 2004)
FARMER, NANCY	*The House of the Scorpion* (Printz Honor 2003)
FREYMANN-WEYR, GARRET	*My Heartbeat* (Printz Honor 2003)
FROST, HELEN	*Keesha's House* (Printz Honor 2004)
GANTOS, JACK	*Hole in My Life* **NF** (Printz Honor 2003)
GOING, K. L.	*Fat Kid Rules the World* (Printz Honor 2004)

GREEN, JOHN	*An Abundance of Katherines* (Printz Honor 2007) *Looking for Alaska* (Printz Winner 2006)
GREENBERG, JAN	*Heart to Heart: New Poems Inspired by Twentieth-century American Art* (Printz Honor 2002)
HARTNETT, SONYA	*Surrender* (Printz Honor 2007)
HEMPHILL, STEPHANIE	*Your Own, Sylvia: A Verse Portrait of Sylvia Plath* **NF** (Printz Honor 2008)
JENKINS, A. M.	*Repossessed* (Printz Honor 2008)
JOHNSON, ANGELA	*The First Part Last* (Printz Winner 2004)
KNOX, ELIZABETH	*Dreamquake: Book Two of the Dreamhunter Duet* (Printz Honor 2008)
LANAGAN, MARGO	*Black Juice* (Printz Honor 2006)
LYNCH, CHRIS	*Freewill* (Printz Honor 2002)
MACKLER, CAROLYN	*The Earth, My Butt, and Other Big Round Things* (Printz Honor 2004)
MCCAUGHREAN, GERALDINE	*The White Darkness* (Printz Winner 2008)
MYERS, WALTER DEAN	*Monster* (Printz Winner 2000)
NA, AN	*A Step from Heaven* (Printz Winner 2002)
NELSON, MARILYN	*A Wreath for Emmett Till* **NF** (Printz Honor 2006)
OPPEL, KENNETH	*Airborn* (Printz Honor 2005)
PARTRIDGE, ELIZABETH	*John Lennon: All I Want Is the Truth, a Photographic Biography* **NF** (Printz Honor 2006)
PLUM-UCCI, CAROL	*The Body of Christopher Creed* (Printz Honor 2001)
RENNISON, LOUISE	*Angus, Thongs, and Full Frontal Snogging: Confessions of Georgia Nicolson* (Printz Honor 2001)

ROSOFF, MEG	*How I Live Now* (Printz Winner 2005)
SCHMIDT, GARY D.	*Lizzie Bright and the Buckminster Boy* (Printz Honor 2005)
STRATTON, ALLAN	*Chanda's Secrets* (Printz Honor 2005)
TRUEMAN, TERRY	*Stuck in Neutral* (Printz Honor 2001)
WITTLINGER, ELLEN	*Hard Love* (Printz Honor 2000)
WOLFF, VIRGINIA EUWER	*True Believer* (Printz Honor 2002)
YANG, GENE LUEN	*American Born Chinese* (Printz Winner 2007)
ZUSAK, MARKUS	*I Am the Messenger* (Printz Honor 2006) *The Book Thief* (Printz Honor 2007)

Author/Title Index

Subject Index

About the Editor and Contributors

Tina Frolund is a librarian in Las Vegas, Nevada. Tina holds a master's degree in library science from the University of Washington, Seattle. She is an active member of YALSA and a reviewer for *VOYA: Voice of Youth Advocates*. Her previous book is *Genrefied Classics: A Guide to Reading Interests in Classic Literature* (Libraries Unlimited, 2006).

Mary Arnold, currently Teen Services Manager for Cuyahoga County Public Library (Ohio), is a former YALSA president. Opportunities to serve YALSA have greatly enriched her professional and personal life, and include chairing Outstanding Books for the College Bound 2004, Margaret A. Edwards Award 2006, and Michael L. Printz Award 2009 Committees. Mary is also a YALSA Serving the Underserved Trainer and Power Up With Print presenter and enjoys sharing a love of teens and reading with colleagues around the country. As a member of NCTE and its Adolescent Literature Assembly, Mary has presented sessions on YA books and authors to English teachers at various national conferences. Publications include articles in *NCTE English Journal*, *The ALAN Review*, YALSA's journal *YALS* on the Margaret A. Edwards Award and YALSA's fiftieth anniversary, and articles on biography and autobiography for teens and crossover reads for the *Continuum Encyclopedia of Young Adult Literature*.

Paula Brehm-Heeger received her MLS degree from Indiana University in 1995. She has worked as a youth services and teen librarian for public libraries in Indiana, Missouri, and Ohio, and has been professionally active on local, state, and national levels for more than a decade. After serving on a variety of committees for the Young Adult Library Services Association, including Teen Advisory Groups, Intellectual Freedom, Popular Paperbacks for Young Adults, and Outstanding Books for the College Bound, Paula was elected YALSA president in 2006. She has written several columns for *The Young Adult Library Services Journal*, is a regular contributor to *School Library Journal*'s "TeenAge Riot" column, and is also a contributor to the forthcoming *YALSA Recommends: Quick and Popular Reads for Teens* (American Library Association, 2008). Her first book, *Serving Urban Teens*, will be published in 2008 (Libraries Unlimited).

Michael Cart is a nationally known expert on young adult literature and a former president of YALSA. During his term, he appointed and chaired the task force that created the Michael L. Printz Award. Subsequently he served as chair of the 2006 Printz Committee. The author or editor of fifteen books, including the young adult novel *My Father's Scar*, Michael is currently a columnist and reviewer for *Booklist*. The author of *From Romance to Realism*, a history of young adult literature, he has taught at UCLA and Texas Woman's University. His most recent books include *Passions and Pleasures: Essays and Speeches About Literature and Libraries* and *The Heart Has Its Reasons: Young Adult Literature with Gay/Lesbian/Queer Content* (coauthored with Christine A. Jenkins). He lives in Columbus, Indiana.

Betty Carter is Professor Emerita from Texas Woman's University, where she taught young adult literature in the School of Library and Information Studies. She has been a YALSA board member, chair and member of the Best Books for Young Adults Committee and the Printz Award Committee, and a member of the Adult Books for Young Adults Task Force. She's written the first two editions of *Best Books For Young Adults* and edited the centennial edition of Margaret Edwards's *The Fair Garden and the Swarm of Beasts*. In addition, Betty and Keith Swigger coedited the *Journal of Youth Services in Libraries* for three years. She is currently a book reviewer for *The Horn Book Magazine*.

Pam Spencer Holley, after teaching biology for seven years, returned to graduate school and earned her MLS from the University of Maryland; she also holds a BS in secondary education from Longwood College, Virginia, and a master's in the teaching of science from the College of William and Mary. Pam worked as a school librarian and eventually became coordinator of school libraries for Fairfax County, Virginia. Her involvement with YALSA began more than 20 years ago. She has chaired Best Books for Young Adults and the Printz Award Committee and will chair the 2009 Odyssey Award committee. A recent term as YALSA president followed a term on the board of directors and a term as YALSA councilor. Writing responsibilities included chairing *School Library Journal*'s "Adult Books for Young Adults" column and the "Audiobooks, It Is!" column for *VOYA: The Voice of Youth Advocates*. Currently Pam writes the young adult summaries for Gale's online subscription database, *What Do I Read Next?*, and has several book projects started for YALSA.

RoseMary Honnold is the young adult services coordinator at Coshocton Public Library in Coshocton, Ohio. A member of YALSA for eight years, she has served on the Teen Read Week Committee and as chair of the jury for the Excellence in Service to Young Adults Award. Starting in 2008, RoseMary will serve as the editor of *Young Adult Library Services*, YALSA's quarterly journal.

RoseMary is the creator of the "See YA Around: Library Programming for Teens" Web site at www.cplrmh.com, has conducted many workshops and conference presentations about library programming for all ages, and is the author of several articles and books, including *101+ Teen Program That Work, More Teen Programs That Work, Serving Seniors: A How To Do It Manual for Librarians, The Teen Readers Advisor*, and *Get Connected: Tech Programs for Teens.*

Erin Downey Howerton is the school liaison for the Johnson County Library in Overland Park, Kansas. She holds an MA in English from Kansas State University and is currently pursuing her MLIS through Florida State University. During the past six years, she has worked with teens and children in various library and educational settings and has obtained certification as a YALSA Serving the Underserved trainer. She is active in the Young Adult Library Services Association, serving on the 2008 Margaret A. Edwards committee and as the editor of *YAttitudes*, YALSA's quarterly e-mail newsletter.